SpringerBriefs in Religious Studies

Springer Briefs in Religious Studies Series is designed to accommodate the growing social scientific research on religion focusing on contemporary issues derived from the challenges of religious diversity, globalization, ethics, law and politics, culture, history, philosophy, education, psychology, society issues, etc. The Series fulfills a scholarly demand for short publications focused on the discussion of new ideas, fieldwork experiences, challenging views, and methodological and theoretical approaches to religion, from a global perspective. The Series will publish innovative social scientific monographs and collections, through a high standard of ethnographic and sociological analysis, which combine scholarly rigor with readable prose for the benefit of scholars and students in various academic fields related to the world of religion. All books to be published in this Series will be fully peer-reviewed before final acceptance.

More information about this series at http://www.springer.com/series/13200

Vivencio O. Ballano

Sociological Perspectives on Clerical Sexual Abuse in the Catholic Hierarchy

An Exploratory Structural Analysis of Social Disorganisation

 Springer

Vivencio O. Ballano
Polytechnic University of the Philippines (PUP)
Manila, Philippines

ISSN 2510-5035   ISSN 2510-5043   (electronic)
SpringerBriefs in Religious Studies
ISBN 978-981-13-8824-8   ISBN 978-981-13-8825-5   (eBook)
https://doi.org/10.1007/978-981-13-8825-5

This Springer imprint is published by the registered company Springer Nature Singapore Pte Ltd.
The registered company address is: 152 Beach Road, #21-01/04 Gateway East, Singapore 189721,
Singapore

This book is dedicated to the Church I love, hoping that it can encourage more scholars to view the current clerical sexual abuse problem from a more sociological and structural perspective.

Preface

The ultimate purpose of this book is to generate more discussions, insights, and sociological studies within the Roman Catholic Church (RCC) to address the current clerical sexual abuse (CSA) in the Catholic hierarchy (CH). It aims to encourage Catholic researchers, theologians, and social scientists to do structural analyses to identify the disorganizing factors which facilitate the persistence of the clerical sexual abuse (CSA) in the CH.

This book is a sociological work. It attempts to provide an empirical assessment of the social structure of the CH as a clerical community with the intention of identifying the social causes of the persistent sexual misconduct of diocesan priests in the Roman Catholic Church (RCC). It neither intends to disrespect priests, bishops, and the Pope with their honest intentions to manage the Church according to Christ's will, nor undermines some of the important canonical and ecclesiastical teachings on the hierarchical structure of the RCC, the primacy of bishops, obligatory clerical celibacy, and lay empowerment. It merely attempts to do a scientific explanation of the structural loopholes in the Church's social organization, social networking, and social control systems in its clerical community, hoping to identify the structural roots of the current clergy sexual abuse and find adequate solutions to prevent sexual misconduct. With positivist training, many sociologists apply value-free judgment when doing a scientific inquiry. They try to bracket their personal biases to see the objective reality. Thus, this study attempts to analyze the social structure of the RCC "objectively" and assess the persistence of the clerical sexual abuse with the "cold neutrality of a judge, "although it acknowledges the ongoing debate on the appropriateness of value-free and value-laden judgments in scientific inquiry.

This book also aims to bring the sociological perspective to the center stage of the debate on the causes of CSA in the RCC. The discourses, views, and researches on why sexual abuses persist in the hierarchy are primarily moral, psychological, and psychiatric in approach. The sociological perspectives which primarily aim to study social systems in a scientific way are apparently sidelined in favor of a more micro and individualist approach in analyzing the causes of CSA. But many empirical studies of this kind have indirectly acknowledged that beyond the personal, moral, and psychological faults of abusive clerics are the social and structural enablers which are left unexplored by social scientists.

The RCC history has a long and continuous documentation of the sexual misconduct by the clergy. Thus, CSA can be considered as embedded in the fundamental social control system of the RCC which tolerates sexual deviance. Clerical sexual scandal in the RCC did not only start in the 1980s with the Boston's Globe investigations of the CSA by clerics in the United States (US). During the early decades of the RCC, there were already been complaints of clerical sexual misconduct, and this type of complaint continues up to the present and shows no sign of letting up and of the capability of the CH to resolve it. So far, it is only the RCC among the many Protestant and Christian Churches which is intensely hounded by this type of abuse worldwide.

The Catholic clerical sexual abuse invites Catholic sociologists to identify the major social disorganizing factors behind its persistence in the CH with the hope that Church authorities would move fast to address them to protect the victims and to rebuild the Church's image. Thus, this book is a modest contribution to this direction.

Manila, Philippines   Vivencio O. Ballano, Ph.D.
                                         Polytechnic University of the Philippines

Acknowledgement

This book on clerical sexual abuse and social disorganization of the Catholic hierarchical community is a product of painstaking sociological research and writing. This journey would not have been possible without the generous help of the following people who prepared and supported me for the task.

To all my Sociology professors of Ateneo de Manila University, for providing me a rigorous training in the sociological enterprise. Special thanks to Dr. Ricardo G. Abad, Professor Emeritus of the Sociology-Anthropology Department at Ateneo de Manila University, my wise advisor and friend throughout my sociological training, for your continuous support and inspiration.

To all my Jesuit Theology professors at the Loyola School of Theology, Ateneo de Manila University, for providing me an in-depth theological formation. Special thanks to the late Fr. John Schumacher, S. J., Fr. Joseph Smith, S. J., and Fr. Romeo Intengan, S. J., for inspiring me to become a scholar and researcher.

To my best friend and former classmate Fr. Dennis Prisco, for providing me some insights on diocesan clerical life and for supporting this book project.

To all my colleagues and co-faculty in the Department of Sociology and Anthropology in Polytechnic University of the Philippines (PUP), for their encouragement and academic support.

To Dr. Nicolas Mallari, Dean of the College of Social Sciences and Development (CSSD) and Prof. Camille Ocampo, Chair of the Sociology Department, at Polytechnic University of the Philippines (PUP), Manila, for their support and encouragement.

To Ms. Alexandra Campbell, my supportive Editor at Springer Nature Singapore, and her team, for their enthusiasm and patience in publishing this book.

To all my students at the Polytechnic University of the Philippines, for their inspiration and encouragement.

To my wife, Emily, and my children, Joanne Faye and Johann Karl, for their loving support and inspiration.

To my sister, Florita O. Ballano, for her generosity and all-out support for all my endeavors and initiatives.

To our Lord Jesus and Mama Mary, for the blessings and guidance in my apostolate of writing—my way of serving the Church and society.

Contents

Abbreviations

CCL	Code of Canon Law
cCSA	Child Clerical Sexual Abuse
CH	Catholic Hierarchy
CSA	Clerical Sexual Abuse
RCC	Roman Catholic Church
SDT	Social Disorganization Theory
US	United States
Vatican II	Second Vatican Council

Abstract

This book, as an exploratory sociological analysis, broadly examines the major structural factors which contribute to the social disorganization of the Catholic hierarchy as a clerical community, facilitating the persistence of clerical sexual abuse in the Catholic Church. Using some tenets of the social disorganization theory on crime and deviance as the overall theoretical framework with some perspectives from social organization, social network, and social capital, and secondary literature and qualitative data to support the arguments, it examines the (1) diocesan clergy's social interaction, mutual support, and social control system in the hierarchical community, (2) connection between mandated clerical celibacy and clerical sexual abuse, and (3) the implication of the laity's lack of empowerment and ecclesiastical authority to monitor and sanction clerical behavior. The Catholic hierarchy prides itself as a unified community of clerics under the Pope who shares the one priesthood of Christ. But the current clerical sexual scandals and the inability of bishops to adequately manage clerical sexual abuse cases make one wonders whether the Catholic clergy is indeed a cohesive and socially organized community which inhibits clerical sexual abuse. This book invites Church authorities, theologians, scholars, and lay leaders to understand the persistent clerical sexual abuse empirically and to come up with structural reforms which enhance the social network and social control systems of the Catholic hierarchy against clerical sexual misconduct and support victims.

Keywords Catholic Church · Catholic Hierarchy · Social Disorganization Theory · Social Control · Clerical Abuse · Catholic Laity

Chapter 1
Introduction

Abstract This chapter discusses the overview of this book. It provides a brief social context of the current clerical abuse of the Catholic clergy in the world. It explains the statement of the problem of the research in which this book is based, as well as the methodology, the review of the related literature, and the theoretical framework in analyzing the persistence of clerical abuse of the secular clergy in the Catholic Church's hierarchy. Finally, it provides a roadmap of the book and summaries of the chapters. Beyond clericalism and psychological causes of clerical sexual abuse, this book argues that sexual misconduct by the Catholic clergy in the Roman Catholic Church has social roots and global dimensions which require a structural investigation into the loopholes in the social interaction and control systems in the Catholic hierarchy as a clerical community.

Background and Statement of the Problem

The clerical sexual abuse (CSA) scandal by members of the Catholic hierarchy (CH) in the United States (US) started in 1984 with revelations about a pedophile priest named Gilbert Gauthe from the Diocese of Lafayette who molested children in the 1970s and 1980s throughout Acadiana as the diocese shifted him from one church to the next (The Acadiana Advocate, 10 Sept 2014). Then a series of investigative reports published by the Boston Globe (2004) had widened this CSA scandal that resulted in an almost hysterical national and international response to the allegations, convictions, resignations, and cover-ups of priest sex offenders. The Globe reports on the molestation of 130 boys by Boston Reverend John Geoghan of the Roman Catholic Church (RCC) from 1962 until 1993 has further exposed the inability of the CH to deal with the problem. The scandal continued in the US with more revelations from investigative bodies and media reports on CSA, fifteen years after the Geoghan scandal.

Recently, Cardinal Theodore McCarrick, the former archbishop of Washington, D.C., was removed from the ministry in June 2018 following allegations that he abused seminarians and young priests in his diocese. He was pinned down with one substantiated case involving abuse of a minor 50 years ago (America, 6 Aug 2018).

Eventually, the Vatican and Pope Francis dismissed McCarrick from the clerical state, a punishment considered as the most severe form of canonical sanction for a cleric (Harlan, 2019). In August 2018, the attorney general in State of the Pennsylvania also released a damning report implicating more than 300 priests in sexual misconduct against more than 1,000 child victims. The release of the redacted report of the state grand jury in the Diocese of Pennsylvania has ignited more fire to the already volcanic issue of CSA in the RCC since 2002. This report which covered six of Pennsylvania's eight dioceses implicated more than 300 priests in CSA cases against more than 1,000 victims in the state from the 1970s and '80s. It further revealed that instead of reporting the CSA to law enforcers, bishops regularly sent abusive clergy to psychiatric assessment and spiritual guidance and then shuffled them from parish to parish, where some would continue to abuse. It reflects the mindset of the CH that CSA is a largely a psychological problem of deviant priests and bishops, rather than a structural problem that has significant organizational causative dimensions that became systematically embedded in Church thinking and practice (Keenan, 2012).

A Snapshot of the Structural and Global Scope of the CSA

The CSA in the RCC is not a recent phenomenon that started only in the US with the Boston clerical scandal in 2002. Doyle (2003) argued that CSA is embedded in the Church's more than 2,000 years of history. He pointed out the steady stream of the Catholic Church's legal documentation, indicating disciplinary pronouncements from popes and the bishops against CSA from the fourth century up to the present day. The current debates in international fora and mainstream media fail to account the historical roots of the Church's awareness of the CSA. They also fail to mention the historic organizational laws that the RCC developed over centuries against clerical sexual misconduct.

The RCC's official documents showed that the Catholic Church did not only a carry century's old history of child clerical sexual abuse (cCSA), but also repeatedly condemn it by successive papal authorities, organizational laws, and institutional management mechanisms. A historical analysis of Rashid and Barron (2018) indicated that the CSA dated as far as the first century and continued up to the end of the 19th century as manifested in organizational laws and institutional policies developed by the RCC to address clerical sexual misconduct up to the end of the 19th century.

Although the sexual abuse scandal involving priests first exploded in the US, reports, stories, and investigations of CSA persist throughout the world. Terry (2015) argued, CSA, especially child clerical sexual abuse (cCSA), by Catholic priests is a global issue. Reports of clerical abuse proliferated in 2002, initially provided the appearance that it was an American phenomenon. But by 2010, with more revelations and investigations on CSA, it became apparent that clergy sexual abuse is also prevalent around the world. Public inquiries and commissions that investigated CSA in other Western and English-speaking countries are ongoing, and similar patterns of abuse and cover-ups by bishops often surfaced in the reports. The CSA is, therefore, not only happening in the US but also in other parts of the globe. No less than Pope Francis himself acknowledged the global scope of the CSA in the CH, prompting him to call for a sexual abuse summit in Rome last February 2019, with more than 200 top Church leaders and clerics from different continents, to address CSA and respond Catholics' call for more concrete actions than simple condemnation.

The CSA problem is not only prevalent in the US but also in Ireland. In a 2,600-page report released in 2009, sexual and psychological abuse was "endemic" in Catholic-run industrial schools and orphanages in the country for most of the 20th Century. Tens of thousands of Irish children were sexually, physically, and emotionally abused by nuns, priests, and others over 60 years in a network of church-run residential schools meant to care for the poor, the vulnerable, and the unwanted (Lyall, 2009).

The RCC in Australia too is facing widespread CSA, especially cCSA. Australia's Royal Commission into Institutional Responses to Child Sexual Abuse, for instance, started its investigations against CSA in 2012. It looked into how the RCC and other institutions responded to sexual abuse of children in the country over 90 years. It heard the testimonies of more than 8,000 survivors of cCSA. Its final report which was released in mid-December 2017, revealed hundreds of cCSA cases and, thus, recommended that the RCC must eliminate mandatory clerical celibacy and abandon the seal of confession when confessions involve child abuse to address the CSA problem (Final Report 2017, pp.731-872). The latest scandal in the Australian Church is the indictment and imprisonment of Cardinal George Pell for molesting two choir boys while he was the archbishop of Melbourne. He was the Catholic Church's highest-ranking official convicted of sexual abuse recently after being appointed by Pope Francis as the Vatican treasurer in 2014. Earlier, Australian Archbishop Philip Wilson became the world's highest-ranking Catholic cleric convicted of covering up cCSA committed by a fellow priest as the Archbishop of Adelaide last July 30, 2018 (Voice of America 12 Feb 2019).

In Europe, Catholic churches also experienced CSA. In Germany, for instance, 1,600 priests and other members of the clergy abused at least 3,677 people between 1946 and 2014, according to a report commissioned by the German Bishops' Conference, with authors conceding that these numbers are probably underestimating the scale of the problem. The report also identified several structures and dynamics within the church that might contribute to abuse, including the requirement of celibacy for priests and the church's rejection of homosexual relationships or practices (NPR 25 Sept 2018). In Italy, which is the home of the Church's papacy, is not spared from CSA. The U.N. Committee for the Rights of the Child, for example, released a critical report in February 2019 about Italy's handling of CSA cases. In its concluding observations on the combined fifth and sixth periodic reports of Italy, the Committee cited its concern "about the numerous cases of children having been sexually abused by religious personnel of the Catholic church in the State party and the low number of investigations and criminal prosecutions" (UN Committee for the Rights of the Child, 1 February 2019).

In Latin America, CSA is also emerging as a serious problem. In Chile, for instance, CSA has also exploded as a public scandal. Thus, Pope Francis summoned Chile's bishops to Rome after receiving a report detailing sexual misconduct by priests in the country. Following an emergency summit, every bishop in Chile offered to resign, an unprecedented action in the modern church (The Catholic Virginian, 18 May 2018). Mexico too is experiencing CSA. On February 10, 2019, shortly before traveling to the papal abuse summit, Archbishop Rogelio Cabrera Lopez, President of the Mexican Bishops' Conference (CEM) announced that 152 Catholic priests had been removed from the ministry over the last nine years for alleged child sexual abuse (BishopAccountability.org, Profile of Summit Attendees).

In Asia, CSA is also growing as a serious threat to the RCC. In the southern Indian state of Kerala, for example, accusations of sexual abuse involving clerics of the CH have demonstrated the challenges of holding some priests and bishops accountable for CSA as clerical pressures often make victims silent. Recently, an Indian court sentenced a senior Catholic priest to 20 years in prison for raping a 16-year-old girl in Kerala. The incident came to light only after the victim gave birth in 2017. Christianity is a minority religion in India, practiced by around 2.3% of the population, and Kerala is home to a sizable Christian community that dates back hundreds of years. Recently, Indian police arrested Catholic Bishop Franco Mulakkal on suspicion of raping a nun 13 times between 2014 and 2016. Mulakkal is now based in the northern state of Punjab and the police have not filed official charges against him (Gupta & Regan, 2019).

The Philippines is the only predominantly Catholic country in Asia with 81.4% of the population identifying as part of the religion (World Atlas [n.d.], Countries with the Largest Catholic Populations). Despite being the largest Catholic country in the continent, cases of clerical sexual misconduct have started to surface as a serious concern for the RCC. In January 2015, for instance, the watchdog BishopAccountability. org collected data on more than 70 accused clergy in the Philippines and published an analysis of twelve key cases involved in CSA. It also identified several Filipino bishops who had dismissed credible warnings about the fitness of their priests. At least seven substantively accused priests were still in active ministry, working openly in parishes or schools. Several others had been banned from US dioceses following serious allegations of child rape and molestation, but still active in the Church ministry. The latest sensational case reported in the media involved a parish priest who was arrested after an attempt to sexually abuse a 13-year-old girl and who sought the services of the victim through a 16-year-old pimp in Marikina City (Philstar, 29 July 2017) and another case involving cCSA of a diocesan priest in the Visayas accused by a mother of molesting her young child. In December 2018, the US Homeland Security agents arrested an elderly American priests on charges that he sexually assaulted at least 7 Filipino altar boys in the rural central Philippines, where he has ministered for decades. At least seven children have come forward, but sources estimate at least 50 cases have been unreported (Gutierrez, 2018).

The CSA scandal is not only limited to cCSA. There are various types of CSA in the RCC that do not involve children. Clerical abuse of children by pedophile priests constitute only around 20% of total sexual abuse by clerics. Rape committed by priests and bishops against nuns, for instance, is also a serious form of CSA in the CH. No less than Pope Francis himself has acknowledged that there are priests and bishops who abuse nuns as sex slaves. Speaking to reporters aboard the papal plane as he returned to the Vatican after a visit to the United Arab Emirates, he mentioned that some of the nuns had been used as sex slaves by some priests and bishops (Buncombe, 2019). He also declared that he suspended a bishop in India who was arrested on September 21, 2018 in the southern state of Kerala on suspicion of raping a nun 13 times between 2014 and 2016. He also revealed that Pope Benedict XVI closed a congregation in France because the founder and its priests treated nuns as sex slaves (Buncombe, 2019).

The February issue of Women Church World, a supplement distributed with the Vatican's Osservatore Romano newspaper, stated that nuns have been silent over abuse by priests for decades for fear of retaliation by some members of the CH. It further revealed that some nuns were forced to abort the priests' children or bear children that the priests refused to recognize. Lucetta Scaraffia, the editor of the magazine, indicated that the clerical abuse of nuns was a global issue and particularly prevalent in Africa, Asia, and Latin America. Reports of such abuse are known to have been made from Chile to the Democratic Republic of Congo, Italy, India, Kenya, Peru, and Ukraine (AFP & Malm, 2019). It also confirmed that the Vatican received reports of priests abusing nuns in Africa in the 1990s.

The RCC's Code of Canon Law (CCL) explicitly condemns sexual abuse by clerics and punish it with canonical sanctions that include suspension and dismissal from the priesthood. Despite these strict sanctions, CSA continues to hound the Catholic Church. A 2017 study released by the Sexual Abuse Royal Commission showed that seven percent of all Catholic priests were alleged perpetrators of cCSA, and the average age of victims was a pre-teen. It also showed that 4,444 people reported incidents of cCSA to 93 Catholic Church authorities from January 1980 to February 2015 (Blackwell, 2017). Despite Pope Francis' latest efforts to reform the Church and enhance the clergy's collegiality, CSA and cCSA by priests, even by bishops continue.[1] Since 2002 the revelations of widespread sexual abuse of minors by Catholic clergy and religious men and women have spread to Europe, Latin America, and to some Asian countries (Doyle, 2012). Clerical sexual misconduct cases continue to emerge in all continents where the RCC is located. The litany of stories and reports of clerical sexual misconduct and cover-ups by bishops continues to grow every day from different parts of the world. Thus, CSA incidents can hardly be considered as isolated cases. It is a growing global pattern in the RCC. Pope Francis himself has acknowledged the global dimension of CSA in a sexual abuse summit held in Rome last February 2019.

With all these growing reports of CSA all over the world, Father Thomas Doyle, an American priest and a well-known advocate against CSA, concluded that sexual abuse by Catholic clergy is one of the greatest crises in RCC history. The CSA scandal has implicated not only priests but also top Church officials for covering up clerical abuse cases. Thus, no one in the CH of the RCC today seems spared from

---

[1] BishopAccountability.org estimated that least 85 bishops around the world have been accused publicly of sexual wrongdoing. But to date, a mere 4 accused bishops have been laicized.

the allegation of either committing or covering up CSA, not even the Cardinals or the Pope.[2]

After the release of the Grand Jury Report on Pennsylvania CSA last August 2018, a former papal ambassador to the US, Archbishop Carlo Maria Vigano, wrote a searing 11-page letter and accused Pope Francis of covering-up the case of Cardinal Theodore McCarrick of Washington, D.C., who have sexually abused a generation of junior seminarians and young priests. It alleged that McCarrick's behavior was an open secret in the Vatican, and yet many high-level officials conspired to promote and keep McCarrick in active ministry (Burton, 2018).

The CSA cases in the US and all over the world involved parish-based clerics and victims from among their congregants (Doyle, 2003). Thus, one wonders why the CH cannot police its ranks: What are the structural flaws in diocesan clergy's way of life that it is prone to CSA? What are the major factors in the Church's social structure and control system which facilitate it?

Popular Approach in the Study of Clerical Abuse

Despite the widespread CSA, not just in the US but also around the globe, the official Church refuses or unable to make any connection between CSA and the internal structural dynamics of the Catholic Church (Doyle, 2006). Bishops and Church officials continue to view sexual abuse in terms of sin, moral fault, and psychological aberration and rely on clinical psychologists and psychiatrists for advice.

To understand the persistence of sexual abuse, many bishops depend heavily on psychological and psychiatric assessments. Several studies also tend to search for psychological factors that cause sexual abuses among the clergy, and ignore the structural and sociological roots of the problem. The 2011 national research commissioned by the United States Conference of Catholic Bishops (USCCB) on CSA–the John Jay College of Criminology study, for instance, largely blames the problematic past and psychological formation of priests and seminarians as encouraging CSA. This is the largest and most in-depth initial study of sex abuse of minors ever carried out by an institution, commissioned by the US Catholic bishops and published in 2004. It found out that over 4% of Catholic clergy in the US had been accused of sexual abuse between 1950 and 2002. And about 80% of the accusations of abuse was alleged to have occurred between the 1960s and the 1980s.

Other studies after this research, which pursue not just the psychological causes but also the cultural roots of CSA, point to clericalism as the enabler of CSA (e.g. Papesh, 2004; Wilson, 2008; Neuhaus, 2017). Shaw (2008) defines clericalism as "an elitist mindset, together with structures and patterns of behavior corresponding to it, which takes it for granted that clerics—in the Catholic context, mainly bishops and priests—are intrinsically superior to the other members of the Church and deserve

---

[2]There were even allegations that Pope Benedict XVI did not act on CSA cases while he was the Archbishop of Munich.

automatic-deference."[3] Clericalism sees the clergy as a privileged class in the Church and gives an impression to the laity that bishops and priests knew best, resulting in the reluctance to acknowledge or report misconduct of priests.[4] The Dominican canon lawyer and scholar Thomas P. Doyle (2006) primarily blames clericalism as the enabler of clergy sexual abuse in the RCC.[5]

But clericalism as an ecclesiastical culture is only a reflection of the social structure of the RCC. The dominance of the clergy in the hierarchical Church breeds a mentality among the other Church members, such as the religious and the laity, that the ordained pastors belong to an elite group of rulers in the Church. The laity considers the clerics as role models in Christian life and spirituality by their imitation of Christ's celibate life and ministry. With the mandated celibacy and lack of lay empowerment in Church governance and the complete separation of the clergy from the laity and religious, diocesan clerics live a less regulated life without direct social control of their personal behavior by spouses and children if married priesthood is allowed. Moreover, the CH would be deprived of stronger indirect social controls that can check clerical deviance without the real empowerment of the laity which could monitor clerical behavior, and allow lay participation in the official decision-making processes of the RCC on CSA cases.

This book aims to examine the structural roots of the persistence of CSA in the CH, particularly in the RCC's diocesan clerical community. It hypothesizes that social disorganization of the CH as a clerical community of pastors with members relatively living independent lives is the primary enable of CSA. It also hypothesizes that the laity is in a position to review clerical behavior in view of their secular vocation. Furthermore, it hypothesizes that the social disorganization of the CH is closely connected with the mandatory clerical celibacy and weak lay participation in the Church management despite Vatican II's renewed doctrine on lay empowerment. Specifically, this book will assess social ties and the bonding system among the members of the CH from the parish up to the Roman Curia and papacy. It will also examine the unintended negative effects of the obligatory clerical celibacy to the social controls of priestly behavior and the implication of having a passive laity in the regulation of clerical behavior and prevention of CSA in the CH.

---

[3]Cited in Richard John Neuhaus, "Clerical Scandal and the Scandal of Clericalism" *First Things,*(March 2008), Retrieved 14 May 2017, https://www.firstthings.com/article/2008/03/clerical-scandal-and-the-scandal-of-clericalism.

[4]Andrew Hamilton. 9 March 2016. "Cultures of Accountability for Priests and Celebrities". *Eureika.com.au*. Retrieved 20 April 2016, https://www.eurekastreet.com.au/article.aspx?aeid=46061#.WQmrWYiGPIU.

[5]Thomas P. Doyle. Clericalism: Enabler of Clergy Sex Abuse. *Pastoral Psychol* 54: 189: 189–213 (2006), https://doi.org/10.1007/s11089-006-6323-x.

The Research Problematic

Clericalism may have contributed to CSA but this could not fully account for the persistence of sexual abuses by secular priests and cover-ups of abuse cases by members of the CH. Clericalism as a clerical culture has structural roots. This elitist view of the clergy as a privileged group and political elite in the ecclesiastical community is only a reflection of the existing Church's social structure that allocates political powers exclusively to ordained clerics. CSA did not only occur in the contemporary era after the media reports on Roman Catholic priests sexually abusing children since the mid-1980s.[6] Sexual abuse of people of any age and either sex by clergy has existed throughout the history of the RCC.[7]

In fact, there is a continuous publication of the RCC's legal documentation indicating disciplinary pronouncements from popes and bishops against CSA from the fourth century up to the present day. CSA can then be seen as embedded in the Church's 2,000-year history,[8] suggesting serious disorganization in the social control system of the RCC against clerical deviance and the hierarchy's capacity to discipline its own clerics and manage sexual abuse cases in favor of the victims. Richard Sipe (1990), the author of the pioneering ethnographic book on clerical celibacy and sexual misconduct, characterized the current CSA as rooted in the Church's ecclesiastical structure. Thus, the CSA problem can be understood as "actually a hierarchy crisis" of the Church itself.[9]

Conversely, clerical sexuality has been shrouded in secrecy for decades. Church authorities usually view CSA as sexual aberrations. Bishops routinely sent to treatment facilities, transferred to different assignments, and settled cases amicably. But this secrecy has been prematurely put to an end when Boston Globe in January 2002 exposed the widespread CSA in the US. And with the intense scrutiny by the media, victims, and grand juries, the structural pattern of widespread sexual abuse by the Catholic clergy gradually emerged.

The Pennsylvania Grand Jury investigation, for instance, which scrutinized six of the state's eight Catholic dioceses in the US, released a report in April 2018 showing the sexual abuse of more 1,000 victims by more than 300 priests over a period of 70 years, including the cover-ups of these cases by bishops and leaders of the RCC. Therefore, what Church officials dismissed as mere psychological aberrations are actually alarming signs of social disorganization in the RCC which tolerates CSA and neglects the proactive monitoring of clerical behavior. The revelation of the widespread CSA in the RCC and the consequent hierarchical mismanagement of

---

[6]P.J. Isley & P. Isley, "Sexual abuse of male children by church personnel: Intervention and prevention" *Pastoral Psychology.* 39. (1990), 85–98.

[7]Thomas P. Doyle, "Roman Catholic Clericalism, Religious Duress, and Clergy Sexual Abuse", *Pastoral Psychology,* Vol 51, No.3, (January 2003), 190.

[8]*Supra,* note 6.

[9]NCR Staff, "Abuse crisis is actually a hierarchy crisis", The National Catholic Reporter, April 10, 2010, Retrieved 24 May 2017, https://www.ncronline.org/blogs/examining-crisis/abuse-crisis-actually-hierarchy-crisis.

cases did not only happen in the US but also in Canada, Australia, New Zealand, Ireland, Scotland, Wales, Great Britain, Mexico, Spain, Poland, Austria, Germany, France, Argentina, and Hong Kong.[10]

The CSA investigations in the US and other parts of the world indirectly provided the public a glimpse of the relatively autonomous lives of diocesan priests and bishops, lacking in communal support and direct and indirect social controls of their behavior in the parishes and dioceses, particularly by the Church's laity. Contrary to Church's claim of clerical communion under the one priesthood of Christ, diocesan priests and bishops relatively live unsupervised private lives, lacking in guardianship and prone to clerical deviance, especially if their spirituality is weak. The RCC is often conceived by the media as a monolithic religious organization, but a closer sociological examination of its social structure reveals a diverse and highly decentralized institution with the CH as a loosely knit clerical network.

The Social Disorganization Theory and CSA

The sociological literature on deviance and crime recognizes the important role of strong social bonding and mutual support in communities to inhibit abusive or criminal behavior. On the one hand, the social disorganization theory (SDT), an established theory in criminology and sociology that started in the 1940s and reemerged in recent decade, hypothesizes that the socially-organized communities exercise a strong social control to keep criminal behavior in check, while the disorganized ones have weak, broken, or ineffective social monitoring of criminal behavior.[11] Social disorganization has been defined by theorists as "the inability of a community to realize common goals and solve chronic problems."[12]

The CH's inability to inhibit clerical abuse and address the enduring clergy abuse can then be seen as serious social disorganization in the diocesan clerical community that warrants a structural investigation,[13] especially on how CSA cases are interpreted and processed by bishops in the diocesan and parish levels. Using the structural analysis method, this book attempts to understand the persistence of CSA in the RCC's CH using the SDT as the overall theoretical framework,

---

[10]Catholics for a Free Choice, the Holy See and the Convention on the Rights of the Child: A Shadow Report 23–28 (2002).

[11]Ronald L. Akers, *Social Learning and Social Structure: A General Theory of Crime and Deviance*: A General Theory of Crimes and Deviance. New Brunswick (USA) and London (UK): Transaction Publishers.

[12]Charis E. Kubrin and Ronald Wiezer, "New Directions in Social Disorganization Theory" *Journal of Research of Crime and Deliquency*. (November 2003), 374–375.

[13]The members of the hierarchy implemented disparate and often conflicting religious and legal responses to clerical sexual abuse in their various roles. See Jo Renee Formicola, "The Politics of Clerical Sexual Abuse," *Religions*. 2016, 7, 9, Retrieved 20 May 2017, www.mdpi.com/2077-1444/7/1/9/pdf, https://doi.org/10.3390/rel7010009.

interspersed with some principles and perspectives from social organization theory (SOT), social network theory (SNT), and social capital theory (SCT).

Methodology

The book's sociological analysis is fundamentally conceptual and exploratory in nature. But it draws on some research studies, secondary literature, and qualitative to support its arguments on the social disorganization of the CH as a priestly community in the RCC. It hypothesizes that the current social disorganization of CH has weakened its social control system to stop the persistent clergy CSA and to handle cases satisfactorily in favor of the victims. Specifically, it uses some Church documents, media reports, as well as anecdotal and qualitative data from interviews of some key informants from one diocese in the Philippines, It also utilizes the memories of the author as a former diocesan and Jesuit seminarian for ten years to support some of its sociological analysis. Since the RCC is a global religious organization in a multicultural environment, the qualitative data and analysis of this book must not be construed as a complete representation of the existing social structure of the universal church but only as an indicator of the general pattern of diocesan clerical life and the CH's attitude towards CSA.

This book is primarily an exploratory structural analysis of the social disorganization of the CH as a community and its implications to the social control of clerical behavior against CSA in the RCC. The SDT is primarily structural in approach, thus fitting to address the structural roots of CSA. "The structural dimensions of community disorganization refer to the prevalence and interdependence of social networks in the community–both informal (e.g. the density of acquaintanceship, inter-generational kinship ties; level of anonymity) and formal (e.g., organizational participation; institutional stability)–and in the span of collective supervision that the community directs toward local problems."[14]

A 'structural analysis',[15] is not a formal theory, but rather a broad strategy for investigating social structures. Thus, its strength lies in its integrated application of theoretical concepts, ways of collecting, and analyzing data. A structural analysis focuses on relational data, on relations between units, rather than sorting units into categories defined by the inner attributes of these units.[16] Aware of the variations of structural or network analysis as well as the limitations of data, this book uses the term structural analysis in the broader sense of doing a macro conceptual analysis using

---

[14]Robert J. Sampson and William Julius Wilson, "Chapter 2, Toward a Theory of Race, Crime and Urban Inequality". *Crime, Race and Justice; A Reader*, (1995).

[15]B. Wellman and S.D. Berkowitz, Structural Analysis in the Social Sciences 2: Social Structures: a Network Approach (Cambridge University Press, Cambridge, 1988).

[16]Barry Wellman, "Structural analysis: from method and metaphor to theory and substance", *Contemporary Studies in Sociology*. Vol. 5, 19–61, Retrieved 9 May 2017, http://homepage.ntu.edu.tw/~khsu/network/reading/wellman2.pdf.

the "sociological imagination" (C. Wright Mills) on the strength of the social ties and social control of the various levels of social network in the Catholic hierarchical community. It utilizes some Church documents, media reports, published researches, and qualitative data based on personal observations and interactions of the author with secular priests and seminarians, unstructured interviews with one diocesan bishop, 10 diocesan priests and 5 former seminarians from two dioceses in the Philippines.

This book explores how the different clerical networks in the CH of the secular clergy from the parish up to the Roman Curia and papacy provide mutual support and behavioral regulation to monitor priestly behavior and prevent CSA. It views the CH as one big community and social network, consisting of three interrelated component networks: the congregational network consisting of the Pope and the Roman Curia, the episcopal network consisting of the various conferences and dioceses around the world, and the parochial network consisting of various parishes within the diocese.

It assumes that a highly cohesive community can produce strong social ties resulting in tighter social controls that can inhibit clerical sexual deviance, while a loose communal network can result in a weak guardianship against CSA. It also assumes that the lack of lay empowerment and the mandatory clerical celibacy, which deprive priests and bishops direct and indirect social control for their personal behavior, contribute to the social disorganization of the CH. The structural sociological analysis of this book on why CSA persists in the CH would center on 3 key areas of social disorganization of the clerical community: (1) the loose social bonding due to lack of sufficient opportunity structure for clerics to enhance the social and spiritual interactions within the clerical hierarchy, from the Pope down to the parish, (2) the negative unintended effect of the mandatory clerical celibacy to the social control of clerical behavior, and (3) the absence of lay participation in the formal governance of the Church, as well as the lack of ecclesiastical authority for the laity to regulate clerical behavior and check CSA.

The Book's Theoretical Orientation

The CSA issue of the CH lacks sociological attention. Most studies which investigate CSA in the RCC tend to focus on the moral, psychological, and psychiatric factors in understanding the persistence of CSA by diocesan clerics rather than on social factors, such as the weak social bonding, social control, and monitoring of clerical behavior. This book examines the literature on the connection between social disorganization and the prevalence of deviance in a community. The sociological literature is replete with theories and research studies on how social disorganization, as well as the weak social bonding, social capital, and social network, can allow the persistence of deviance and criminal behavior in organizations. But sociological literature which investigates the social causes of CSA is apparently lacking. This book, therefore, aims to fill this gap.

Although this book is primarily using some tenets of the SDT as the main theoretical framework, it also utilizes some theoretical insights from other related theories such as the social network, social organization, and social capital. The main concern of this book is to theorize the structural causes of the persistent CSA in the RCC. The SDT fundamentally focuses on the relationship between neighborhood structure, social control, and crime. But recent research work has refined the formulation of the theory.[17] To apply the SDT in analyzing the cohesiveness of the CH and its capacity to monitor clerical behavior, the book's structural analysis would attempt to apply the three intervening constructs of the theory; namely, the (1) rate of participation of the members in formal and voluntary organizations within the community; (2) strength of local ties to increase guardianship against victimization; and the (3) presence of supervise groups within the community to strengthen social control mechanism.[18] These constructs will be supplemented by some theoretical contributions of other network and social organization perspectives.

The book's analysis would utilize the first construct by investigating broadly the opportunity structure of the CH which promotes the social and spiritual bonding between priests in the parish level, bishops and their priests in the dioceses, as well as between bishops and Pope and Roman Curia in Rome, and between bishops worldwide. In the second construct, it examines the strength of social control and monitoring systems in the dioceses and parishes which determine the strength of guardianship against clerical deviance. In the last construct, it investigates the presence of supervising groups in the RCC against CSA and the unintended disorganizing effects of mandatory clerical celibacy and the weak lay participation in ecclesiastical governance and behavioral regulation of clerics in the CH. Overall, it hypothesizes that the low social cohesion and weak social control system of the Catholic hierarchical community, despite the RCC's claim of clerical unity, are the primary social disorganizing factors that fuel the persistence of CSA in the Church.

Social Disorganization and Deviance

The interconnection between a loose communal bonding of community members and the prevalence of deviance has a long theoretical and research tradition in Sociology. In his classical theory on anomie, Emile Durkheim, for instance, theorized that isolated people lack social ties to society that inhibit them to commit crimes. The feeling of alienation and state of 'normlessness' can push isolated individuals to commit deviance.[19] Even criminologists before and after Durkheim have attempted

---

[17]Charis Kubrin and Ronald Weitzer, 2003. "New Direction in Social Disorganization Theory" *Journal of Research in Crime and Delinquency.* Vol 40, Issue 4, pp. 374–402. https://doi.org/10.1177/0022427803256238.

[18]Robert J. Sampson and Byron W. Groves, "Community Structure and Crime: Testing Social Disorganization Theory. *American Journal of Sociology* 92, no. 4, 774–782. Reprinted in Frances Cullen and Velmer Burton, eds., Contemporary Criminological Theory. Dartmouth Publishing Co., 1994.

[19]J. A. Fagin, *Criminal justice introduction to criminal justice college of public safety.* New Jersey: Prentice Hall, (2010).

to find the cause of crime not in the personal traits of individuals but in such external factors as population density, economic conditions, natural forces, and ecological areas (Glick & Miller, 2007).

The use of SDT to identify the cause of crime and deviance became popular in the 1940s with the work of the early Chicago-research school scholars. Shaw and McKay (1942), for instance, studied the high delinquency rates in certain Chicago neighborhoods and concluded that: it is the ecological conditions that primarily shaped crimes rates over and above the characteristics of individual residents.[20] This classical ecological explanation, however, fell out of flavor in subsequent years and reemerged in the past two decades with the reformulation of the theory, starting with the seminal works of Kornhauser (1978), Stark (1987), Bursik (1988), Sampson and Groves (1989), and Bursik and Grasmick (1993).[21]

In the 80s, social disorganization and the study of the role of communities in individual crime (contextual analyses) and crime distributions (aggregate level of analyses) returned on the research agenda. The Crime and Justice volume Communities and Crime (Reiss & Tonry, 1986) contributed by bringing together a new generation of academics with a renewed interest in (Chicago) community research, not just by mimicking the insights of Shaw and McKay, but by posing new research questions. Since then, a revival of disorganization studies emerged in the US, extending classic disorganization perspectives with other structural indicators and intervening processes such as social cohesion, informal control, social trust, social ties, social capital, and collective efficacy (Bruisma, Pauwels, Weerman, & Bernasco, 2013, p. 4).

Recent research on social disorganization has taken two distinct but related directions. These have been referred to as the systemic model of social disorganization (Bursik & Grasmick, 1993, 1996) and the social capital/collective efficacy framework developed by Robert Sampson and his colleagues (Sampson, Morenoff, & Earls, 1999; Sampson, Raudenbush, & Earls, 1997). With these works, the SDT is now focused on the informal social control and the collective ability of neighborhoods to intervene and supervise residents to maintain public order (Sampson et al., 1997, 1999). It assumed that the weakening of informal control mechanisms can disable neighborhoods to control crime.[22]

Social disorganization has been defined as "the inability of a community structure to realize the common values of its residents and maintain effective social controls" (Kornhauser, 1978:63). Empirically, the structural dimensions of social disorganization are measured by scholars in terms of the prevalence and interdependence of social networks in the community–both informal (e.g. friendship ties) and formal (e.g. organizational participation)–and in the span of collective supervision that the

[20]Charis E. Kubrin and Ronald Wiezer, "New Directions in Social Disorganization Theory" *Journal of Research of Crime and Deliquency.* (November 2003), 374–375.

[21]Charis E. Kubrin and Ronald Wiezer, "New Directions in Social Disorganization Theory" *Journal of Research of Crime and Deliquency.* (November 2003), 374–375.

[22]Fred E. Marcowitz, et al., "Extending Social Disorganization Theory: Modeling the Cohesion between Relationships, Disorder, and Fear". Criminology 2, 9, (May 2009), 293–294.

community directs toward local problems (Thomas & Znanaiecki, 1920; Shaw & McKay, 1942; Kornhauser, 1978).[23] To Bursik (1988), Sampson & Wilson (1995), Sampson & Groves, (1989) the real meaning of social disorganization is the absence or breakdown of informal social control. The socially organized neighborhoods or communities are expected to exercise strong social control to keep deviant and criminal behavior in check. But those which are disorganized have weak, broken, or ineffective social control and less able to contain crime in a community or neighborhood.[24]

Under the social disorganization perspective, the network indicators most consistently associated with crime reflect the size of local family and friendship networks (Kapsis, 1976, 1978; Sampson & Groves, 1989; Simcha-Fagan & Schwartz, 1986), organizational participation (Greenberg et al., 1982; Kapsis, 1976; Sampson & Groves, 1989; Simcha-Fagan & Schwartz, 1986), disorder (Simcha-Fagan & Schwartz, 1986; Skogan, 1990), and the extent of local consensus and cohesion (Kapsis, 1978; Maccoby et al., 1958; Warren, 1969). These studies suggest that social networks centered around the family, close friendship ties, and community organizations, are effective agents of social control.

A socially organized community is characterized by (1) solidarity, or an internal consensus on essential norms and values (e.g., residents want and value the same things, such as a crime-free neighborhood); (2) cohesion, or a strong bond among neighbors (e.g., residents know and like one another); and (3) integration, with social interaction occurring on a regular basis (e.g., residents spend time with one another). Conversely, a disorganized community has little solidarity among residents and lacks social cohesion or integration. Perhaps the greatest difference between socially organized and disorganized neighborhoods is the levels of informal social control in those neighborhoods. Informal social control is defined as "the scope of collective intervention that the community directs toward local problems, including crime" (Kornhauser, 1978; Shaw & McKay, 1969; Kubrin & Wo, 2016, p. 122).

> In essence, residents act as the 'eyes and ears' of the community and their informal surveillance, and even simple presence, deters others from engaging in crime. According to the theory, socially disorganized neighborhoods have lower levels of informal social control, and thus experience higher crime rates when compared to more socially organized neighborhoods (Kubrin & Wo, 2016, pp. 122–123).

While social control is absolutely central to social disorganization theory, virtually all writers focus on informal control, which includes "private control" (within primary groups) and "parochial control" (exercised through interpersonal networks and local community groups) (Bursik & Grasmick, 1993). What is largely missing

---

[23]Robert J. Sampson and Byron W. Groves, "Community Structure and Crime: Testing Social Disorganization Theory". *American Journal of Sociology* 92, no. 4, 774–782. Reprinted in Frances Cullen and Velmer Burton, eds., Contemporary Criminological Theory. Dartmouth Publishing Co., 1994.

[24]Ronald L. Akers, *Social Learning and Social Structure: A General Theory of Crime and Deviance*: A General Theory of Crimes and Deviance. New Brunswick (USA) and London (UK): Transaction Publishers.

is the examination of formal control, which refers to practices of the authorities to maintain order and enforce legal and regulatory codes. Informal control is important because it is community-based and thus more central in mediating the neighborhood characteristics on crime, whereas institutions based outside the neighborhood exercise formal control. Informal control can as more likely to prevent crime than formal control with the authorities, which often takes place after the fact. But the neglect of formal control is problematic for social disorganization theory. Formal control may be important in two ways: (1) by directly influencing crime and disorder and (2) by influencing residents' informal control practices (Kubrin & Weitzer, 2003, p. 8).

Although social control is largely discussed in many social disorganization studies, formal social control is a missing part of this theory. For Kubrin and Weitzer (2003), formal control is functional in both directly alleviating crime and disorder, and influencing the informal control capacity of the residents in a neighborhood (p. 382). Without formal control mechanisms, when community action is needed, the intervention of community members will not take place due to reluctance or fear of victimization. Formal control through policing is also of great importance in terms of maintaining social control. This book will argue that the CH of clerics lacks formal social control or policing of clerical behavior as the RCC lacks a professional judicial system which effectively checks CSA and prosecutes erring priests for sexual misconduct.

Social Organization and Social Disorganization Perspectives

One of the central tenets of social disorganization theory is the idea of social control. According to the original contributors of social disorganization theory, namely: Charles H. Cooley, W. I. Thomas, Florian Znaniecki, and William F. Ogburn, cultural conflict and breakdown of social control in communities are the root causes for social disorganization (Rubington & Weinberg, 2010, pp. 52–55). Although the concept of social control is important in SDT for the prevention of crime in communities or organizations, its root is actually found in social organization perspectives.

SDT shares with the social organization theory (SOT) in the idea of social control. Social organization is understood as "the collection of values, norms, processes, and behavior patterns within a community that organize, facilitate, and constrain the interactions among community members" (Mancini, Martin, & Bowen, 2003, p. 319). It is the process by which communities achieve their desired results for individuals and families, including the ability of individuals and families to demonstrate resiliency in the face of adversity and positive challenge. It includes networks of people, the exchanges and reciprocity that transpire in relationships, accepted standards and norms of social support, and social controls that regulate behavior and interaction.

Social organization is often seen by scholars as suppressing community problems such as crime, delinquency, or child maltreatment (Freisthler, 2004). Social organization is historically connected with the social disorganization theory of delinquency

(Kornhauser, 1978). Thus, social organization theory (SOT) and SDT can be viewed as opposite ends of a continuum that reflected a community's ability to control problems (Cantillon, Davidson, & Schweitzer, 2003).

A recent review by Sampson et al. (2002) is an important contribution to understanding social organization processes, particularly through research on neighborhood effects. Sampson et al. (2002) organized neighborhood-level process variables into four categories: (a) social ties and interaction, (b) norms and collective efficacy, (c) institutional resources, and (d) routine activities. At the individual level, process-oriented variables include prosocial activities, social ties with neighbors, daily hassles, and social activities. The SOT has a particular value for opening up the "black box" between the social structure and the results experienced by individuals and families in communities: (a) formal and informal social networks, (b) social capital, and (c) community capacity. These social organizational processes are dynamically and reciprocally interrelated and combine in additive and interactive ways to influence individual and family outcomes.

On the one hand, SDT emphasizes the importance of indirect social controls in communities and neighborhoods to prevent crime and deviance. Social control is an effect of strong social ties and networks of members of a community. Informal control has been traditionally theorized as an outcome of social ties (Bursik 1988, p. 527). It provided by factors removed physically from the person, such as institutions, traditions, customs, and culture. Sampson and Groves (1989) stressed the importance of informal social control, which is sustained by the internal dynamics of a community and define social disorganization as the failure of a community in sustaining common values, and in maintaining effective social controls in the community.

On the other hand, SOT emphasizes direct social control as crucial in the social organization of communities to achieve its goals and values. It works when someone exerts influence on a person directly due to their close proximity such as members of one's immediate family. Direct social control is 'visible' but indirect means of social control are 'invisible and subtle' (Sharma, 2007, p. 221).

This book views the crucial role of social control in the Catholic hierarchy's capacity to address and prevent CSA. Mandatory celibacy, as shown in the Chap. 4, for instance, can take away direct social control which provides direct guardianship and monitoring of the cleric's behavior. It also deprives clerics of informal social networks created by a married priesthood which can improve the cohesion of the CH and inhibit clerical deviance. As shown in Chap. 5, the lack of lay empowerment and participation in the internal management of the Church also weakens the social control system in the Church, particularly the power of the laity to directly monitor and sanction clerical deviance and create intermediary lay support groups within the CH if married priesthood becomes an option and universal practice in the RCC.

Social Network and Social Capital Perspectives

Two theories which can enhance the SDT's structural analysis of persistent crimes in organizations and communities concerning social cohesion and networking of the various elements of an organization or community are the social network theory (SNT) and social capital theory (SCT).

The SNT stands part of the social science theory because it focuses on the social context and behavior of relationships between actors rather than on the rational choices individual actors make, as seen in disciplines such as economics and the social and decision sciences (Fredricks & Durland, 2005). The SNT traditions did not evolve into a coherent theoretical framework until the 1960s. A number of sociologists significantly advanced the social network approach by synthesizing previous theoretical traditions and extending them to understand both formal and informal social relations (Liu, Sidhu, Beacom, & Valiente, 2017, p. 1).

The SNT focuses on the joint activities of and continual exchanges between, participants in a social system. This perspective is characterized by an interest in the recurrent relationship patterns that connect the actors that make up a system's social structure (Kenis & Oerlemans, 2009). Probably the single most important concept in a social network approach is the relationship among actors, which can be individuals or groups such as organizations or parts of organizations. Rather than examining actors in isolation, the SNT sees actors as embedded within networks of interconnected relationships that provide opportunities for, as well as constraints on, behavior. The focus is on the interaction between actors rather than on their attributes as actors, such as size (Liu et al., 2017).

The key components of a social network approach are actors, ties and dyads, ego-centric network, complete network, positional properties of actors in networks, and structural properties of networks. Actors in networks, also called nodes or vertices, can be persons or teams, organizations, countries, regions, and so on. In the field of inter-organizational relations, these ties are also called relations, lines, or edges. Dyadic ties connect pairs of actors and define the substantive relationships that exist between the ego (the focal organization) and alters (those related to ego). They can range from friendships and social contacts to formal contracts, working relationships, giving and/or receiving advice, interlocking directorates, etc. The social network perspective represents a move 'away from individualist, essentialist and atomistic explanations toward a more relational, contextual and systematic understanding' (Borgatti & Foster, 2003: 991).

Fewer long-standing relationships among members of a community can result in weaker social ties, less social capital, and thus poorer quality resources (Warner, 1999). A social tie is a relationship to a potential resource. It can be a strong tie (close, frequent relationship) or a weak tie (i.e., a distant and infrequent relationship). Social capital is most commonly defined as both the actual and potential resources embedded in social ties that can be used to achieve an outcome. Two of the previously identified achievement gap categories were individual psychological characteristics and school quality. Research has shown how individual behaviors and development result from the quality of social ties (Madyun, 2011, p. 24).

Thus, another theory which can help the SDT's interest in social network perspectives against crimes in communities is the Social Capital Theory (SCT). This theory is widely seen as popularized by Pierre Bourdieu in 1985 (Portes, 1998), Coleman in 1988, and Putnam in 1993 (Portes, 1998). Bourdieu explained social capital as aggregates of resources related to permanent or transitory social networks (Portes, 1998). To him, social capital is instrumental for individuals in the sense that they participate in building social networks as well as pursuing their interest in return to their endeavors. Social capital has two dimensions: First, the individual access of resources through their relationships, and second, the quality of resources. Therefore, the utility provided by social capital to the members is also the basis of a social network (Portes, 1998).

Social capital is, in the most general sense, a measure for an actor of the value of his social connections. Although it underlies the importance of relations between actors, mainly from a resource perspective, social capital itself can also be considered from a more genuine social network perspective. Both Burt (1992) and Coleman (1990) have introduced a topological view of social capital that emphasizes the importance of the interconnections among the members of a whole network. Berger and Murphy (2000) also underline the importance of informal social control maintained by social capital. As a result, better families, strongly knit neighborhoods, and decent occupations provide better opportunities for social capital to community members. Contrarily, neighborhoods with lower social capital will produce an unpleasant living environment (p. 48). Social capital emerges through the building of relations among persons, which promotes the ability to act for the utility of all individuals (Coleman, 1988, p. 100).

Social Disorganization Theory and Clerical Abuse

This book attempts to utilize some important theoretical tenets of the SDT as the overall analytical framework to analyze the persistence of CSA in the hierarchy of clerics in the RCC, supplemented by some theoretical concepts from the SNT, SOT, and SCT to widen the book's structural analysis.

Although the SDT is often used to understand crimes in urban neighborhoods and communities, some scholars attempted to relate it to religious organizations and sexual abuse. Dina Rose (2000), for instance, studied the relationship between social disorganization and parochial control, particularly whether more disorganized communities support fewer religious institutions. Specifically, her study explored the relationship between religious institutions and multi-issue neighborhood-based organizations.[25]

---

[25]Rose, Dina R. "Social Disorganization and Parochial Control: Religious Institutions and Their Communities." *Sociological Forum* 15, no. 2 (2000): 339–358. http://www.jstor.org/stable/684819.

What is closer to the issue of clerical sexual abuse in churches is the dissertation study of Andrew Denney (2015), which used the social disorganization theory to examine sexual offenses in Protestant churches. This study created a typology of offenders and victims in Protestant churches in the US. Although it some provided valuable information to scholars and practitioners on a rarely examined topic of sexual abuse in Christian churches, it did not focus on the social cohesion of Protestant churches and its effect to the supervision of sexual deviance by church ministers.[26]

Despite the nuances in the formulation of the theory, the SDT's three intervening substantive dimensions can be used to evaluate the level of cohesiveness of the CH in the RCC and its effects to clerical abuse. The first important intervening construct is the strength of social ties within the different social networks in a community as crucial in maintaining a socially organized community. When members of the community form local social ties, their capacity for social control increases because they can recognize strangers and more apt to engage in guardianship behavior against victimization (Skogan, 1986, p. 216). The idea of social ties as crucial in social control primarily comes from the social network (SNT perspective which this study utilizes to supplement the SDT. Strong social ties as crucial in social control is acknowledged in SNT) for delinquency causation which also highlights the importance of network density to prevent deviance. A network density is the extent to which all actors in a social network are connected by direct relations. When network density is high, the ability to control delinquency is increased because the behavior of the participants in such a network is potentially subject to the reactions of all network members (Khron, 1986).[27]

Another significant intervening construct which will be utilized in this book informally is Shaw and McKay's (1942) theoretical model which sees the ability of the community to supervise groups within the community as significant to curb crime. The capacity of the community to control group-level dynamics is a key mechanism linking community dynamics with delinquency. This implies that a community which has a higher level of supervision over their different groups is more likely to control deviant behavior than the one with low supervision. In this case, this book would investigate the judicial and social control systems in the CH as a clerical community and assess how the various clerical networks or levels of authority in the RCC support and supervise each other to check clerical abuse. This implies utilizing some insights on social control which is central in the SOT.

The third important construct is the rate of local participation in formal and voluntary organizations in the community. Community organizations reflect the structural embodiment of local community solidarity (Hunter, 1974, p. 191), and, in his mind, Kornhauser (1978, p. 79) argues that institutional instability and the isolation of community institutions are key factors underlying the structural dimension

---

[26]Denney, Andrew Stephen, "Sex offenses at Protestant Christian churches: a typology and examination using social disorganization theory." (2015). Electronic Theses and Dissertations. Paper 2102. https://doi.org/10.18297/etd/2102.

[27]R.J., Bursik Jr. and H.G. Grasmick, *Neighborhood and Crime.*Lexington, MA: Lexington Books, (1993).

of social disorganization. Here, some theoretical insights from SOT, SNT, and SCT are also utilized in the chapters of the book's structural analysis. In the RCC, this construct implies revisiting mandatory clerical celibacy and giving importance to familial networks that support the stressful life of diocesan priesthood as well as providing greater authority and participation of the Catholic laity in monitoring and supervising the clerical behavior of the CH. Social disorganization theorists suggest that to solve common problems such as predatory victimization, communities must have high rates of participation in committees, clubs, local institutions, and other organizations which can lower rates of victimization and delinquency.[28]

Applying these three constructs with some theoretical insights from SOT, SNT, and SCT, the structural analysis of this book is divided into three major parts. The first part examines the spiritual and social interaction of the CH as a religious and human community. Specifically, it broadly investigates the opportunity structure for spiritual formation and social interaction between bishops, Roman Curia, and Pope, between bishops and their priests, and between priests in the dioceses. The second part examines the RCC's and judicial system for clerical behavior in the different component networks of the CH from Pope down to the parish priests. And the last part analyzes the social disorganizing effects of the universal celibate priesthood and weak participation of the Catholic laity in the formal and informal social controls of the clerical community. Categorically, it analyzes the active role of the laity in the church governance such as lay advisory boards and pastoral councils in providing additional intermediary social networks, social controls, and guardianship against CSA.

Judging Clerical Abuse in the Church

The RCC as a complex religious institution in society does not only have a legal code but also a myriad of intertwining doctrinal, ethical, sacramental, and moral normative standards that affect ecclesiastical decision-making and behavior. Thus, local ordinaries or bishops face a variety of normative considerations in judging CSA. Without a clear hierarchy of judicial authority, the inconsistent and conflicting applications of the Church's normative standards to specific CSA cases are not automatically subject to judicial review.[29]

The RCC has given the bishops more ecclesial powers to settle local CSA cases. The Vatican seldom interferes with bishops' discretion in deciding cases of their

---

[28]Robert J. Sampson and Byron W. Groves, "Community Structure and Crime: Testing Social Disorganization Theory". *American Journal of Sociology* 92, no. 4, 774–782. Reprinted in Frances Cullen and Velmer Burton, eds., Contemporary Criminological Theory. Dartmouth Publishing Co., 1994.

[29]The lack of a professional judicial system in the Catholic Church is a major cause of delay in the investigation and prosecution of abuses committed by priests. See Nicolas N. Cafardi, *"Before Dallas: The U.S. Bishops' Response to Clergy Sexual Abuse of Children"*. New York: Paulist Press, (2008).

priests unless these cases erupted into public scandals such as the sexual abuses of priests in the US that attracted the attention of the Roman Curia and Pope. With multiple norms and religious teachings to apply to individual cases, the bishops' decisions may not always follow the Church's canonical provisions and people's judicial expectations strictly.[30] To local ordinaries, legality is not the only criteria for the CH in deciding cases; it also include and, ultimately, the unity of the Church as one Body of Christ. The RCC's response to CSA undergirds the belief that criminal abuse by clergy should be sanctioned by the Church internally—if at all—under canonical commands of contrition and forgiveness, and not by civil authorities.[31]

Many American bishops, for instance, believed that their supervision of the clergy, even in sexual abuse situations, was an internal supervisory matter to be handled by them, a traditional ecclesiastical right protected from state intrusion by historical religious exemptions to civil law. Therefore, they relied either on the Church's legal system, the Code of Canon Law, to adjudicate allegations of CSA or their own personal interpretations of Church norms to punish the priests under their control, without effective lay participation. This approach gives bishops more discretionary power on how to judge and address clerical abuse and disables them to develop a systematic method, indicating normative pluralism in judging clerical abuse despite the Canon Law provisions against it (Formicola, 2016, p. 3). Thus, the state's version of legality based on a professional judicial system is not the absolute standard for the RCC to judge CSA—to the dismay of the victims and the general public. The social disorganization of the CH in addressing the CSA is fundamentally connected with the laity's lack of authority to participate in the decision-making processes of the official Church in sanctioning CSA, resulting in many cover-ups of abuse cases by bishops and top clerics who may use a plurality of formal and informal norms to justify their decision to protect the image of the Church and personal interests.

The Book's Roadmap

The overall objective of this book is to understand the persistence of CSA in the CH primarily using the social disorganization perspective. Specifically, it examines how the following three areas contributes to the social disorganization of the primarily as a priestly community: the social bonding of clerics and supervision of clerical behavior within the various levels or social networks of the hierarchy, the obligatory clerical celibacy and the consequences of a weak laity in the internal management of the RCC as well as the surveillance and sanction of clerical behavior.

---

[30] Canon law is the official statute of the Catholic Church. It includes the Code of Canon Law and many other canonical documents issued by Popes, Roman Congregations, Bishops' Conferences and Bishops. The current ecclesiastical code in the Catholic Church is the Code of Canon Law for the Latin Church was promulgated on January 25, 1983, and went into effect on the First Sunday of Advent that same year (Daly, 2009, p. 33).

[31] Wayne A. Logan, "Criminal Law Sanctuaries", *Harvard Civil Rights-Civil Liberties Law Review*, Vol 38, (2003), 321.

Chapter 1 provides an overview of the book. It discusses the background of the study and research problem in which this book is based, methodology, review of the related literature, and theoretical orientation in analyzing the persistence of CSA by the secular clergy in the Catholic Church's hierarchy. It also explains the significance of the book and summarizes the book's chapters.

Chapter 2 broadly examines how the weak and infrequent social interaction of the clergy in the CH can lead to social disorganization that weakens the hierarchy's internal social control against CSA. It also provides an overview of the composition, social interaction, spiritual formation, and networking of the CH in the parish, diocese, episcopal conference, Roman Curia, and papacy, and their consequences to clerical behavior and social control. In particular, it aims to show how the loose structural bonding of the secular clergy in the various communal levels of the CH and the apparent lack of direct and direct social controls provided by lay organizations in the various levels of the clerical community, can lead to a weak social cohesion, mutual support, and social control of clerical behavior against CSA in the hierarchical community of the clergy.

Chapter 3 broadly analyzes the social cohesion of the CH as a clerical community. It investigates the supervision and coordination of the various clerical networks of the hierarchical community from Pope and the Roman Curia down to the lowest network of the parishe and draws some implications to the social control of clerical behavior against sexual abuse. It argues that the weak social bonding of the various networks and primacy of college of bishops as a clerical network in the CH contributes to the social disorganization of the Catholic clergy and the persistence of CSA in the Church.

Chapter 4 discusses the crucial role of the family and universal married priesthood in the social control of clerical behavior and prevention of clerical deviance. It draws on some empirical studies to stress the social disorganizing factor of mandatory celibacy to the communal life of the CH against CSA. It argues that the universal obligatory celibacy with its culture of clericalism deprives secular clergy of direct guardianship against CSA, given the general lack of intimacy and social bonding among priests and between priests and their bishops in dioceses and parishes. Living a relatively autonomous life, diocesan clerics find themselves without strong direct and indirect social controls offered by marital and family relations and obligations. The SDT recognizes the crucial role of social bonding and intimate groups in monitoring and preventing deviant behavior in social disorganized communities such as the CH.

Chapter 5 analyses the role of the laity in the social organization of the CH as a community of clerics and the social control of clerical behavior against CSA. It stresses the need for stronger lay empowerment in the social control and behavioral monitoring of the secular clergy by allowing the laity to participate in the formal governance of the RCC. It also examines the renewed teaching of the Second Vatican Council (Vatican II) on lay empowerment and participation in the Church and reevaluates it whether it constitutes substantial lay empowerment which can result in the formal sharing of ecclesiastical power and authority between the clergy and the laity check and prosecute CSA. It argues that real political empowerment of the laity can improve the social organization of the RCC against CSA.

Summary

This chapter has provided an overview of the book in terms of the social context, research problematic, method, theoretical framework and review of related literature on CSA. It views the persistence of CSA as rooted in the very structure of the CH itself as a loosely knit clerical community, lacking in social cohesion and social control against clerical deviance. Using some important concepts and principles of the SDT as an overall framework of the book, with some theoretical insights from SOT, SCT, and SNT, it aims to present five chapters to examine the three factors or areas that contribute to the social disorganization of the CH, namely: the autonomy of clerical life in the various levels of the clerical hierarchy, universal celibacy, and the weak lay participation in the Church governance.

References

AFP & Malm, S. (2019) Editor of Vatican's women's magazine says 'many' rape claims have been filed with the Church 'but not followed up' as she praises Pope for admitting priests kept nuns as 'sex slaves'. *MailOnline*. Retrieved February 6, 2019, from https://www.dailymail.co.uk/news/article-6674227/Editor-Vaticans-womens-magazine-says-claims-priests-raped-nuns-ignored-Church.html.

America (2018, August 6). The editors: The Catholic Church should not be shocked by the McCarrick case—it should be ashamed. *America*. Aug. 62018 Issue. Retrieved December 22, 2018 from https://www.americamagazine.org/faith/2018/07/17/editors-catholic-church-should-not-be-shocked-mccarrick-case-it-should-be-ashamed.

Becker, G. S., & Murphy, K. M. (2000). *Social economics: Market behavior in a social environment*. England: Harvard University Press.

Blackwell, E. (2017). 7 percent of all catholic priests were alleged sex abuse perpetrators: Royal commission. Retrieved May 14, 2017, from http://www.huffingtonpost.com.au/2017/02/05/catholic-church-under-royal-commission-spotlight/.

Boncumbe, A. (2019). Pope admits sexual abuse of nuns by priests in Catholic Church for first time. *The Independent*. Retrieved 6 February 6, 2019, from https://www.independent.co.uk/news/world/europe/pope-francis-nuns-sexual-abuse-catholic-church-priests-scandal-bishops-a8765031.html. (Accessed 28 February 2019).

Borgatti, S. & Foster, P. (2003). The Network paradigm in organizational research: A review and typology. *Journal of Management*. 29(6), 991—1013

Bruisma, G., Pauwels, L., Weerman, F., & Bernasco, W. (2013) Social disorganization, social capital, collective efficacy and the spatial distribution of crime and offenders: An empirical test of six neighbourhood models for a Dutch city. *British Journal of Criminology, 53*(5), 942–963.

Bursik, R. J. (1988). Social disorganization and theories of crime and delinquency: Problems and prospects. *Criminology 26*, 519—551.

Bursik, R. J., & Grasmick, H. G. (1993). *Neighborhoods and crime*. New York: Lexington.

Bursik, R. J., & Grasmick, H. G. (1996). Neighborhood-based networks and the control of crime and delinquency. In H. Barlow (Ed.), *Crime and public policy* (pp. 107–130). Boulder: Westview Press.

Burt, R. S. (1992). *Structural holes*. Cambridge, MA: Harvard University Press.

Burton, T. I. (2018). Ex-Vatican official accuses Pope Francis of covering up McCarrick's sex abuse. *Vox*. 27 Aug. 2018. Retrieved September 3, 2018, from https://www.vox.com/2018/8/26/17783168/pope-francis-vigano-cover-up-accusation-sex-abuse.

Cantillon, D., Davidson, W. S., & Schweitzer, J. H. (2003). Measuring community social organi-
    zation: Sense of community as a mediator in social disorganization theory. *Journal of Criminal
    Justice, 31,* 321–339.
Chaskin, R. J., Brown, P., Venkatesh, S., & Vidal, A. (2001). *Building community capacity.* New
    York: Aldine De Gruyter.
Coleman, J. S. (1988). Social capital in the creation of human capital. *American Journal of Sociology,
    94*(1), 95–120.
Coleman J. (1990) *Foundations of social theory.* Cambridge, MA: Belknap Press of Harvard Uni-
    versity Press.
Daly, B. (2009). Sexual abuse and canon law. *Compass, 43*(3), 33—40.
Doyle, T. P. (2003). Roman Catholic clericalism, religious duress, and clergy sexual abuse. *Pastoral
    Psychology, 51,* 189.
Doyle, T. P. (2006). Clericalism: Enabler of clergy sex abuse. *Pastoral Psychology, 54,* 189–213.
    https://doi.org/10.1007/s11089-006-6323-x.
Doyle, T. P. (2012). Sexual abuse in the Catholic Church: A decade of crisis, 2002–2012: A radical
    look at today and tomorrow. Retrieved May 17, 2017, from http://www.awrsipe.com/Doyle/2012/
    Santa%20Clara%20-%20May%2015,%202012c[5].pdf.
Greenberg, S., W., Rohe, W. M., & Williams, J. R. (1982). *Safe and secure neighborhoods: Physical
    characteristics and informal territorial control in high and jaw crime neighborhoods.* Washing-
    ton, D.C.: National Institute of Justice.
Final Report (2017). Religious Institutions: Volume *16,* Book 2. *Royal Commission into Institutional
    Responses to Child Sexual Abuse.* Available at: https://www.childabuseroyalcommission.gov.au/
    sites/default/files/final_report_-_volume_16_religious_institutions_book_2.pdfhtml.
Formicola, J.R. (2016). The politics of clerical sexual abuse. *Religions, 7*(1), 9.
Freisthler, B. (2004). A spatial analysis of social disorganization, alcohol access, and rates of child
    maltreatment in neighborhoods. *Children and Youth Services Review, 26,* 803–819.
Fredericks, K. A. & Durland, M. M. (2005), The historical evolution and basic concepts of social
    network analysis. New Directions for Evaluation, 15—23. 10.1002/ev.158.
Glick, L. & Miller, J. M. (2007). *Criminology* (2nd). Boston: Allyn & Bacon.
Gupta, S., & Regan, H. (2019). Catholic Church's problems with abuse are playing out in India
    amid summit. *CNN Style.* Retrieved February 22, 2019, from https://edition.cnn.com/2019/02/
    21/india/india-catholic-church-abuse-intl/index.html.
Gutierrez, J. (2018). American priest accused of molesting boys in the Philippines. *The New
    York Times.* Retrieved December 6, 2018, from https://www.nytimes.com/2018/12/06/world/asia/
    american-priest-molest-boys-philippines.html.
Harlan, C. (2019, February 16). Ex-cardinal McCarrick defrocked by Vatican for sexual abuse.
    Washington Post.
Hunter, A. (1974). *Symbolic communities: The persistence and change of chicago's local commu-
    nities.* Chicago: Chicago University Press.
Keenan, M. (2012). *Child sexual abuse and the Catholic Church: Gender, power, and organizational
    culture.* Oxford and New York: Oxford University Press.
Kapsis, R. (1976). Continuities in Delinquency and Riot Patterns in Black Residential Areas. *Social
    Problems, 23,* 567—580.
Kapsis, R. (1978). Residential Succession and Delinquency. *Criminology* 15, 459—486.
Kenis, P., & Oerlemans, L. (2009) The social network perspective: Understanding the struc-
    ture of cooperation, The Oxford handbook of inter-organizational relations. Oxford Hand-
    books Online. Retrieved March 2, 2019, from http://www.oxfordhandbooks.com/view/10.1093/
    oxfordhb/9780199282944.001.0001/oxfordhb-9780199282944-e-11.
Khron, M.D. (1986). The web of conformity: A network approach to the explanation of delinquent
    behavior. *Social Problems ,* 33(6), 81—93.
Kornhauser, R. R. (1978). *Social sources of delinquency: An appraisal of analytic models.* Chicago:
    University of Chicago Press.

Kubrin, C., & Weitzer, R. (2003). New directions in social disorganization theory. *Journal of Research in Crime and Delinquency, 40*(4). https://doi.org/10.1177/0022427803256238.

Kubrin, C. & Wo, J. (2016). Social disorganization theory's greatest challenge: Linking structural characteristics to crime in socially disorganized communities. In Piquero, A. R. (ed). *Handbook of Criminological Theory*, 1st ed, New Jersey: John Wiley & Sons.

Lyall, S. (2009). Report details abuses in Irish dormitories. *New York Times.* Retrieved May 20, 2009, from https://www.nytimes.com/2009/05/21/world/europe/21ireland.html. (Accessed 1 March 2019).

Liu, W., Sidhu, A., Beacom, A. M., & Valiente, T. W. (2017). Social Network Theory. In P. Rossler, C. A. Hoffner, & van Zoonen (Eds.), The International Encyclopedia of Media Effects. US: Wiley.

Maccoby, E., Johnson, J., & Church, R. (1958). Community integration and the social control of juvenile delinquency. *Journal of Issues* . 14, 38—51.

Madyun, N. H. (2011). *Connecting social disorganization theory to African-American outcomes to explain the achievement gap.* Summer-Fall 2011: Educational Foundations.

Mancini, J. A., Martin, J. A., & Bowen, G. L. (2003). Community capacity. In T. P. Gullotta & M. Bloom (Eds.), *Encyclopedia of primary prevention and health promotion* (pp. 319–330). New York: Kluwer Academic/Plenum.

Neuhaus, R. J. (2017). The scandal of clerical abuse and the scandal of clericalism. *First Things.* Retrieved May 14, 2017, from https://www.firstthings.com/article/2008/03/clerical-scandal-and-the-scandal-of-clericalism.

NPR (2018, September 25). German bishops' report: At least 3,677 minors were abused by clerics. Retrieved December 22, 2018, from https://www.npr.org/2018/09/25/651528211/german-bishops-report-at-least-3-677-minors-were-abused-by-clerics.

Papesh, M. L. (2004). *Clerical culture: Contradiction and transformation: The culture of the diocesan priests in the United States Catholic Church.* Collegeville, Minnesota: Liturgical Press.

Philstar Global (2017, July 29) Priest nabbed for trafficking minor in Marikina. *Philippine Star Gobal.* https://www.philstar.com/metro/2017/07/29/1722768/priest-nabbed-trafficking-minor-marikina.

Portes, A. (1998). Social capital: Its origins and applications in modern sociology. *Annual Review of Sociology, 24*(1).

Putnam, R. D. (1993). The prosperous community: Social capital and public life. *American Prospect, 13*(4), 35–42.

Rashid, F., & Barron, I. (2018). The Roman Catholic Church: A centuries old history of awareness of clerical child sexual abuse (from the first to the 19th century). *Journal of Child Sexual Abuse, 27*(7):1–15.

Rubington, E., & Weinberg, M. S. (2010). *The study of social problems: Seven perspectives* (7th ed.). New York: Oxford University Press.

Reiss Jr., A.J. & Tonry, M. (eds) (1986). *Communities and Crime.* Chicago: Chicago University Press.

Sampson, R. J., & Groves, W. B. (1989). Community structure and crime: Testing social-disorganization theory. *American Journal of Sociology, 94,* 774–802.

Sampson, R. J., Raudenbush, S. W., & Earls, F. (1997). Neighbourhoods and violent crime: A multi level study of collective efficacy. *Science, 227,* 916–924.

Sampson, R. J., Morenoff, J. D., & Earls, F. (1999). Beyond social capital: Spatial dynamics of collective efficacy of children. *American Sociological Review, 64,* 633–660.

Sampson, R. J., Morenoff, J. D. & Gannon-Rowley, T. (2002). Assessing 'neighborhood effects': Social processes and new directions in research. *Annual Review of Sociology, 28,* 443—478.

Sampson, R. J., & Wilson, W. J. (1995). Toward a theory of race, crime, and urban inequality. In J. Hagan & R. D. Peterson (Eds.), *Crime and inequality* (pp. 37—54). California: Stanford University Press.

Sharma, K. (2007). *Social Changes and Social Control.* New Delhi: Atlantic Publishers & Distributors (P) Ltd.

Shaw, R. (2008). *Nothing to hide: Secrecy, communication, and communion in the Catholic Church*. San Francisco, USA: Ignatius Press.

Shaw, C. & McKay, H. (1942). *Juvenile Delinquency and Urban Areas*. Chicago: Chicago University Press.

Shaw, C. & McKay, H. (1969). *Juvenile Delinquency and Urban Areas*, rev. ed. Chicago: Chicago University Press.

Simcha-Fagan, O. M., & Schwartz, J. E. (1986). Neighborhood and delinquency: An assessment of contextual effects. *Criminology, 24*(4), 667—699.

Skogan, W. (1986). Fear of crime and neighborhood change. In A. J. Reis, Jr. & M. Tomry (Eds.) *Communities and Crime*, pp. 203—209. Chicago: Chicago University Press.

Skogan, W. (1990). Disorder and decline: Crime and the spiral of decay in american neighborhoods. Berkeley, CA: University of CA Press.

Stark, R. (1987). Deviant Places: A Theory of the Ecology of Crime. *Criminology, 25*, 893—909.

Terry, K. J. (2015). Child sexual abuse within the Catholic Church: A review of global perspectives. *International Journal of Comparative and Applied Criminal Justice, 39*(2), 139–154. https://doi.org/10.1080/01924036.2015.1012703.

The Catholic Virginian (18 May 2018). All of Chile's bishops offer resignations after meeting pope on abuse. Available at: https://www.catholicvirginian.org/?p=7496.

Thomas, W. I. & Znaniecki, F. (1920). *The Polish Peasant in Europe and America*, Vol. 4. Boston: Gorham.

Voice of America (2019, February 27). Australian Cardinal convicted of child sexual abuse taken to jail. *Voice of America*. https://www.voanews.com/a/australia-clergy-abuse/4805669.html.

Warner, B. D. (1999). Whither poverty? social disorganization theory in an era of urban transformation. *Sociological Focus, 32*(1), 99—113.

Warren, D. I. (1969). Neighborhood structure and riot behavior in detriot: Some exploratory findings. *Social Problems*. 16, 464—484.

Wilson, G. B. (2008). *Clericalism: The death of priesthood*. Collegeville, Minnesota: Liturgical Press.

World Atlas (n.d.). *Countries with the Largest Catholic Populations*. Available at: https://www.worldatlas.com/articles/countries-with-the-largest-catholic-christian-populations.html.

Chapter 2
Catholic Hierarchy and Social Interaction of the Clergy

Abstract This chapter provides an overview of the composition, social interaction, spiritual formation, and networking of the Catholic hierarchy in the parish, diocese, episcopal conference, Roman Curia, and papacy, and their consequences to clerical behavior and social control against clerical sexual abuse. Particularly, it aims to show how the loose social structural bonding of the secular clergy in the various communal levels of the hierarchy and the apparent lack of formal and informal controls provided by lay organizations in the various levels of the clerical community can facilitate clerical abuse.

Introduction

The Catholic hierarchy (CH) as a community of pastors is spatially dispersed throughout the world. The Supreme Pontiff and clerical members of Roman Curia, the highest governing body of the Roman Catholic Church, (RCC) reside in Vatican City. The different archdioceses and dioceses, as well as parishes, are found in different parts of the universal church. This geographical dispersion of the clergy does not necessarily mean an absence of priestly communion in the various clerical networks of the RCC from the parish churches up to the Roman Curia and Pope. The RCC assumes that all members of the CH form a communion, a closely knit religious community which is linked spiritually by one priesthood of Christ and under the guidance of the Pope (Canon 880-885).

The RCC's Code of Canon Law (CCL) affirms the unity and communion of all bishops and ordained ministers of the Church as constituting one college or community under the leadership of the pope (Canon 883): "Just as by the Lord's decision Saint Peter and the other Apostles constitute one college, so in a like manner the Roman Pontiff, the successor of Peter, and the bishops, the successors of the Apostles, are united among themselves" (Canon 330). But to what extent are members of CH united in actual social practice?

The CH as a human and spiritual community is one big religious network of deacons, priests, and bishops all over the world under the leadership of the pope in Rome. Despite the affirmation of ecclesiastical documents concerning the communion and social cohesion of all clerics as participating in one ministerial priesthood of Christ, empirical research and sociological investigation into this alleged unity and communion remain lacking. With the current clerical sexual scandals that hound the RCC worldwide, one wonders whether the CH is indeed cohesive enough as a community to police its ranks against the crime of clerical sexual abuse (CSA). Sociological studies investigating the density of the social network and behavioral regulation of the CH against CSA is apparently absent, thus this sociological study.

Factors external to individuals usually shape crimes such as CSA in sociological approaches. Sociological theories on crime in communities, for instance, recognize the necessity of a strong social cohesion of all members within an organization to generate stronger social controls to overcome crime and deviance. The social control theory (SCT), for instance, sees crime as a result of social institutions losing control over individuals. Weak institutions such as certain types of families, the breakdown of local communities, and the breakdown of trust in the government and the police, are all linked to higher crime rates. Hirschi (1969), the main proponent of SCT, argued that criminal activity occurs when an individual's affiliation to one's community in terms of attachment, commitment, involvement, and belief is weakened. Moreover, acknowledged the crucial role of social bonding and network for the inhibition crime in a community.

Some studies have demonstrated a relationship between social capital and reductions in crime (Chalin and Cochran 1997; Rosenfeld et al. 2001; Messner et al. 2004). Putnam (2000) defines social capital as referring to "connections among individuals—social networks and the norms of reciprocity and trustworthiness that arise from them" (p. 19). He distinguishes two types of social capital: bridging capital and bonding social capital. The former is linked to what network researchers refer to as "weak ties," which are loose connections between individuals who may provide useful information or new perspectives for one another, but typically not emotional support (Granovetter, 1982). Alternatively, bonding social capital is found between individuals in tightly knit and emotionally close relationships, such as families and close friends. Social capital provides the glue which facilitates co-operation, exchange, and innovation. Communities and regions with higher levels of social capital tend to have healthier citizens (Putnam, 2000). Other research has also demonstrated social capital's effectiveness at reducing crime (Rosenfeld, Messner, & Baumer, 2001), victimization of crime (Hawdon & Ryan, 2009), firearm violence (Kennedy, Kawachi, Prothrow-Stith, Lochner, & Gupta, 1998), and fear of crime (Kruger, Hutchison, Monroe, Reischl, & Morrel-Samuels, 2007). The level of social capital in a neighborhood can be linked to crimes through social disorganization.

The social disorganization theory (SDT) is one of the sociological theories on crime which aims to explain the endurance of deviance in large communities. The breakdown of social bonds, associations, social controls in families, neighborhoods, and communities can result in what Thomas and Znaniecki (1958) termed "social disorganization." Social disorganization is popularly defined as the "the inability of a community structure to realize the common values of its residents and maintain effective social controls" (Kornhauser, 1978:63). The SDT became popular in the

1940s with the work of the early Chicago-research school scholars (e.g. Shaw & McKay, 1942). It is also utilized as a theoretical framework by some scholars in ethnographic studies to investigate crimes and clerical abuses in religious communities and organizations, although this theory usually investigates criminality in urban communities and neighborhoods using census data. Residents in socially disorganized neighborhoods will not act on suspicious behavior because it is viewed as none of their concern. The withdrawal from the social institutions in a disorganized neighborhood leaves residents with little recourse in attempting to stop antisocial behavior (Moore & Recker, 2013, p. 731).

An important area of SDT in understanding the persistence of crime is the strength of the social bonding and network cohesion of the various members and groups in a community. Kapsis (1976, 1978), for instance, suggested that frequent social interactions among community members minimize the incidence of crime. He found that neighborhoods where a larger proportion of the residents interacted on a weekly basis and perceived a consensus within the community experienced less crime and deviance.

A long-standing assumption of the social disorganization perspective is that frequent forms of interaction are the most important means to inhibit crime. Residents or members of a community who maintain social ties with neighbors may be willing to engage in guardianship and supervision of public space within a neighborhood even if they do not consider others as close friends (Bellair, 1997). Occasional interaction may increase the ability of neighborhood residents to engage in informal surveillance of public places, to develop movement-governing rules such as avoiding high-risk areas, engaging in direct intervention by questioning residents and strangers about any unusual activity, and admonishing children for their unacceptable behavior (Bursik, 1988).

To know whether a community has elements of social disorganization requires an inquiry into the opportunity structure of the social interaction of different groups and individuals within a community. It also includes an examination of the "bridging social capitals" (Putnam, 2000) or intermediary networks that connect the various levels of the community to increase social ties and guardianship against crimes. This chapter examines the social interaction structure of the Catholic diocesan clergy and analyzes whether it is sufficient to develop strong social ties and social control against CSA. It first examines the composition of the CH and then the frequency and quality of social interaction of secular clerics.

The Composition of the Catholic Hierarchy

The CH as a clerical community is composed of the pope, bishops, priests, and deacons who exercise authority within the Church (CCC #874-879). The RCC members are generally classified into three groups: The clergy which constitutes the CH, the religious who professes religious vows in the RCC, and the laity who is baptized, but neither professes vows nor receives ordination. The hierarchy refers to the clergy or ordained ministers of the RCC who profess vows of celibacy and obedience. The religious are religious priests, brothers, and active or contemplative nuns who profess vows of poverty, chastity, and obedience, and live in religious orders or congregations. The laity is the largest group of baptized members with no vows in the RCC. Despite the Church's insistence on unity, equality, and sharing of one priesthood of Christ by all members, a distinction of social status between these three types of members is often observed in the universal RCC.

The ordained ministers of the CH are always considered by the Code of Canon Law (CCL) as the exclusive rulers of the RCC (Canon 274,1). The pope is the sign of unity of the CH and overall head of the college of bishops, clerics, and deacons (CCC, 882). Although they occupy larger dioceses and territorial jurisdictions, the cardinals and archbishops are also bishops who exercise the same powers and duties of local ordinaries. Cardinals as bishops have additional duties of advising the pope on Church matters and electing a new pope (Canon 349). The deacons occupy the lowest position in the hierarchical community assist the diocesan clergy by performing some of the sacraments (CCC, 1554). They can either be transitional deacons or seminarians studying for the priesthood or permanent deacons who can be ordained as married laymen.

The CH as a clerical community has an opportunity structure that is assumed by Church authorities as adequate to enhance their spiritual and social communion. But the persistence of CSA in the RCC puts this assumption into question and necessitates a structural inquiry into the frequency and quality of social and spiritual interaction of the various clerical groups in CH and its consequences to priestly behavior—whether clerics, indeed, live a strong cohesive community that polices its members against CSA. More frequent and intimate interactions supported by a stable structure can generate strong social controls against crime. The SDT assumes that irregular and impersonal or contractual interactions among members of a community can result in social disorganization and weak resistance against crime.

Seminary Formation and Parish Structure of the Clergy

The RCC as an evolving and expanding religious organization has various communities and social networks with different cultural expressions in the world. Despite the cultural diversity and plurality of Christian communities within the universal RCC, the clerical community remains a "special type of community" within the multiple communities of the universal Christian community. The RCC started with a small band of disciples and apostles of Christ in Israel. With more 2,000 years of history, it gradually grew from a small group of Jewish believers of the risen Christ concentrated in one small country into a global organization with more one billion members around the world and governed by a small but powerful group consisting exclusively of ordained clerics with Pope as the overall leader. The RCC is cleric -centered. Despite the Second Vatican Council's (Vatican II) renewed teaching on lay empowerment, the dichotomy between clerical and lay communities in the Church is still rigid. The clerical community which consists only of less than one percent of the Church's population is looked up to with high esteem by Catholics as pastors and political leaders of the RCC. The CH gives special attention to the priestly training and community structure of clerics in seminaries and parishes. Despite the perceived Christian unity of all communities and social networks in the RCC such as religious orders, congregations, third orders, lay institutes, basic ecclesial communities, mandated parish organizations, and monastic communities, the clerical community of CH often seen by Catholics as the "political elite" of the RCC and, thus, given a special preference by the Church authorities in terms of priestly formation and organization.

But similar to other Catholic organizations within the universal organization of the RCC, the seminary and parish organizations underwent a long history of organizational growth, adjustment or what institutional theorists call as isomorphism and decoupling. A long standing question in organizational research is what makes organizations more or less similar to each other. Early organization theorists pointed out that organizations which share the same environment tend to take on similar forms as efficiency-seeking organizations to seek the optimal 'fit' with their environment. Institutional theories of organization have added two related claims: First, organizations adapt not only to technical pressures but also what they believe society expects of them, which leads to institutional isomorphism. Second, when adaptations to institutional pressures contradict internal efficiency needs, organizations sometimes claim to adapt when they in reality do not; they decouple action from structure in order to preserve organizational efficiency (Boxenbaum & Jonsson, 2008, p. 78).

Seminary Formation Through the Years

The seminary formation of clerics as it exists today did undergo isomorphism and decoupling as organizations within the RCC. A central idea of isomorphism is that organizations conform to rationalized myths in society about what constitutes a proper organization, while decoupling implies changing, separating or reforming of organizations to adapt to the environment and preserve organizational efficiency (Boxenbaum & Jonsson, 2008). In the RCC's apostolic tradition, the general sentiment of the Christian community, and the so-called "signs of the times" as interpreted by the CH in ecclesiastical councils serve as a guide for any reform within the universal and local organizations of the RCC. The long history of priestly formation and parish structure have passed through many phases in response to the Church's council directives to read the "signs of the times" and listen to pastoral demands of the Christian community.

The three years Jesus spent with his apostles is sometimes referred to as the first "seminary program. Jesus is the first formator of priests with the twelve disciples as the first seminarians. But this informal and face-to-face type of priestly training did not persist today as the Catholic population increased through time and the clerical community became bureaucratized. There was no formal priestly training during the first four centuries. The popular priestly formation during this period was apprenticeship with local bishops or parish priests. This practice continued until the twelfth and thirteenth centuries when university programs with residential life and a rigid regimen of compulsory devotions and "demanding asceticism" for priests were established in response to "the sorry moral condition of the clergy" (Schuth, 2016).

Over a period of nearly twenty years (1545–1563), the Council of Trent addressed many issues related to the clergy and decreed that every diocese must establish colleges solely for priestly training. The decree emphasized the theological and ascetical training for diocesan priests based on the model of the risen Christ as priests and victims. The intention of this decree on seminaries was to protect 'endangered youth' by removing them from the world and to fortify them in their priestly vocation (Schuth, 2016). Thus, priestly formation became monastic. Seminaries became isolated from the world to shield priestly candidates from worldly temptations. Thus, seminaries, like monasteries, are usually located in remote places, away from the secular affairs of the city.

Vatican II, a universal council which was convened by Pope John XXIII in October 1962 to modernize the RCC and adapt it to the globalizing world challenged and reformed the monastic approach to seminary formation. Its official documents have had a profound impact on the life of the church, especially its decree on seminary formation– *Optatam Totius* (Decree on the Training of Priests). Issued on October 28, 1965, four hundred years after the Council of Trent's document on priestly formation, this new document revolutionized seminary formation and required numerous adjustments in seminaries (Schuth, 2016, p. 3). Vatican II moved away from the monastic approach to seminary formation to a more pastoral one, allowing the establishment of seminaries near urban centers and allowing lay students to join seminarians in clerical education.

Until the 1970s, most seminaries closely resembled with those prescribed by the Council of Trent's 1563 decree on seminaries. Leaders made few substantial changes after Vatican II, though by the mid-1960s some authors began writing about modifications and adaptations in design and method for seminary formation. To most Catholics, even after the mid-twentieth century, seminary training seemed enclosed and impenetrable. But much of what had transpired in seminaries for four hundred years changed radically in 1965 with the publication of *Optatam Totius*. This document continues to influence seminaries and pastoral formation programs for both seminarians and lay students up to the present era (Schuth, 2016, pp. 9–10).

Seminary formation under the Council of Trent and Vatican II provided a strong and cohesive communal life for candidates in the priesthood. With the regimented life inside the seminary, the behavior of seminarians is closely monitored by priests and formators which inhibit deviance and sexual abuse. But this cloistered and regulated life ends when the seminarians are ordained as priests. The social structure of the parish life does not provide the regimented life offered by the seminary for newly ordained priests. The parish is fundamentally structured meant to provide spiritual services to the faithful and the assigned priests are presumed to have internalized the personal and spiritual discipline during the seminary formation.

The Parish Structure

Canon 515.1 of the Code of Canon Law (CCL) describes the parish as "a defined community of the Christian faithful established on a stable basis within a particular church." In the fourth century, when Christianity in Western Europe spread to the countryside, Christians in an important village were organized into a unit called the parish under a parish priest and bishop of the nearest city. Pastoral care is the principal distinguishing feature of parochial organization—what might be considered in modern times as the delivery of religious rites such as baptism, marriage, communion or burial. The frequency of the delivery of services and geographical location of the parish is perceived to be crucial for the parish church. Until the nineteenth century, people lived in a world where matters of distance and location were determined largely by walking distances (Zech & Gautier, 2004, p. 142).

The diocesan bishop appoints the parish's pastor leader, whether a priest or someone else. Aside from their importance as communities of the faithful, parishes are also juridic persons under Canon 515, 3. This means that they have legal personalities just as a business partnership or a corporation does in the secular legal system. As a result, only the diocesan bishop has the authority to create, suppress, or otherwise alter a parish (Zech & Gautier, 2004).

Vatican II which modernized the RCC in the 1960s had a major impact on parish organization. One outcome is the development of awareness of what it means to be a church. The Decree on the Apostolate of the Laity describes the laity as the people of God. Because of this, lay people are more willing to assume parish management roles. Even without the decline of priests, expanded pastoral activity of lay people in the parish based on Vatican II emerged (Zech & Gautier, 2004). Despite this development, the parish as the lowest social network in the hierarchical community did not evolve into as a small intimate community which provides mutual support for diocesan priests.

Unlike the seminary, the parish is structured as the center for the delivery of religious services to Catholic believers in urban and rural areas. In many smaller parishes, only one priest is assigned and in some cases, due to the shortage of priests, he\has to administer the sacraments to two or more parishes. In big parishes of Catholic countries such as the Philippines, an urban parish can accommodate one parish priest and more than one assistant priests or pastors. Guest priests can stay for a short period and help in providing spiritual services to the faithful. Bit increased membership of clerics in a big parish does not necessarily results in greater intimacy and social cohesion of the clerical members.

The parish church is not primarily designed by the RCC as a clerical community with more members, communal activities, and regimented way of life. Unlike a seminary where the behavior of seminarians is always supervised by formators, the parish church has no surveillance system which can monitor or regulate the behavior of the parish priest or whoever is assigned as pastors. Only the bishop, who is often not in constant contact with his several diocesan priests, has the power to discipline clerical misconduct. Unlike religious priesthood, the diocesan priesthood offers no regular and frequent communal activities for clerics which can cultivate mutual support and strong social bonding, necessary to inhibit clerical abuse or sexual misconduct.

The significant difference in the social structure between the regimented life of the seminary and the absence of clerical communal activities and absolute privacy of clerical behavior in the parish is the reason why newly ordained priests often encountered personal crisis and loneliness during the first five years in the ministry. The transition from seminary life to active ministry is often difficult fro young priests. The newly ordained diocesan priests who get used to be surrounded by friends and formators in the seminary suddenly become lonely after ordination, especially when assigned in remote parishes or where there is an age gap between them and their older parish priests.

The Clerical Social Networks in the Hierarchy

The community of the Catholic clergy is hierarchical. It consists of various levels of clerical networks, depending on the power and authority of the ordained ministers. The lowest level in the clerical social network is the parish network consisting of diocesan priests and deacons in one diocese under the leadership of the bishop. Ideally, each parish church has one parish priest as the pastor with one or more priests acting as assistant pastors, especially in large parishes. A parish is "a certain community of Christ's faithful stably established within a particular Church, whose pastoral care, under the authority of the diocesan Bishop, is entrusted to a parish priest as its proper pastor" (Canon 515).

The first clerical network can be the community of diocesan priests. This network is the college of priests or presbyterium, governed by a presbyteral council and the bishop (Canon 495, 1). The second level of the clerical network is the college of bishops in a national conference, such as the Catholic Bishops' Conference of the Philippines (CBCP). This community of bishops in an episcopal conference is usually located in one country or region. The College of Cardinals is another level of social network consisting of top clerics in the RCC who are tasked to advise the Supreme Pontiff and elect a new pope. Finally, the fourth and highest network, which is often called as the Holy See, is the highest clerical network consisting of the top Church administrators who are clerical members of the Roman Curia who are directly under the supervision of the pope.

Although the RCC speaks about collegiality of the clergy in the CH, such as those in the Vatican headed by the Pope and bishops, or between bishops and priests, frequent social interactions among clerics to foster personal and spiritual intimacy seldom supported by the social structure. The hierarchy remains a less cohesive\community with a lack of lay intermediary groups and organizations which can provide direct and indirect social controls to deter CSA. With the complete separation between the clergy, religious, and the laity in the Church membership structure and imposition of mandatory celibacy, the CH appears lacking of what Putnam (2000) calls as bridging social capital in between the major social networks of the clergy. Because the laity cannot exercise political powers in the official Church, there are no lay intermediary organizations and networks between parishes and dioceses, and between dioceses and the Holy See. The prevailing clerical networks which coordinate the major networks are limited and controlled only by clerics, resulting in weak overall social network of the CH. One hallmark of socially disorganized communities is the lack of intermediary networks which is necessary to strengthen social ties and social controls against crime.

The Social Interaction of Priests in the Parish Network

The lowest level of the clerical social network of the CH is the parish network consisting of a small community of diocesan priests in one big parish' otherwise the parish priest lives alone in the parish church. A person becomes a diocesan priest after long years of seminary training in Philosophy and Theology and receiving ordination from his bishop. Once ordained, he usually becomes an assistant parish priest, and then appointed as the parish priest, depending on the pastoral need and discretion of the bishop or local ordinary.

Diocesan priests relatively live an autonomous life in the parish community. They can be lonely and isolated in the parish without the friendly companionship of their fellow priests. Despite the Church's pronouncements that priests live in communion with one another, the structural interaction of the clerical community is limited due to the 'atomistic' structure of the parishes in the diocese and lack of a communal system that allows frequent and intimate interaction among diocesan priests. Unlike religious priests, diocesan priests do not have a regimented communal life. They do not have regular daily communal prayers and set of activities that can promote strong social bonding similar to their former seminary training. The camaraderie that has been established during the seminary years could no longer be sustained after ordination as newly ordained priests are assigned to various parishes, oftentimes assigned with older priests as their parish priests. After ordination, young priests are usually designated by their bishops in parishes and become detached from their former classmates, friends, and schoolmates in the seminaries who used to serve as their intimate support groups.

A study of Cornelio (2012) on priesthood satisfaction confirmed that new priests can become lonely in the parishes because of their detachment from their seminary friends as aptly illustrated by the feeling of loneliness of Fr. Robert:

> [T]he separation from my previous life in the seminary where I was in the company of other seminarians. Suddenly I am now alone in the parish. Sometimes I look for people I can talk to but I only have two neighbors in the parish. So why does he not talk to them? Of course

I talk to them but I have other daily duties in the parish. So most of the time I only see my secretary. So I don't have any variation in my life in the parish.[1]

One informant of another study (Clancy, 2008) revealed the difficulty of the newly ordained priests to adjust to the age gap with their fellow priest. Bill, a newly-ordained priest complained:

> I think maybe for me the one transitional problem that I might have had is going from a larger group of individuals that you live with and kind of having that sense of camaraderie here and there is, but it's not the same, because they're not, I like the pastor but he is my father's age. The senior priest is my grandfather's age. When I was at St. John's there were guys my age and I think being around guys my age is something I miss.

The key informants of the study also admitted loneliness after ordination and confirmed that they became were detached from their former seminary friends and formators. So the real test to the priest's life is really after ordination, on how to live a priestly life which lacks social bonding with their fellow priests in the parishes and away from prying eyes of their superiors.

The social structure of the clerical ministry which provides more freedom for priests in their private lives is totally different from the more controlled environment of the seminary. Experts who had handled personal crises of priests confirmed the isolated life of diocesan priests. One experienced psychologist-therapist of priests for 30 years aptly described the solitary life of young priests:

> The real challenge comes after ordination when the observing eyes of superiors are far away. Over the past 30 years, the number of priests has been going down dramatically. Young priests are often sent to parishes alone after minimal on-the-job training with an older colleague.

> This can be heady, exciting, frightening, anxiety-producing, and even intoxicating. It is also easy in this context to feel lonely, misunderstood, and powerfully desirous of solace beyond the purely spiritual kind… It is common in priest circles to find reasons for things, and there are usually plenty on offer as to why an ordained priest would forsake his vows and get involved with a woman (to take the obvious case) or with another man: frustration, disappointment, loneliness, experiencing one's self as sexual once the microscope of training has ended — even the freedom a man experiences being on his own (Midden, 2016).

One major problem of seminary formation is that it largely imparts informally male camaraderie: team sports, guys socializing, and guy group activities. But once the seminarian is ordained as a priest, this strong sense of intimacy or belonging to a community suddenly disappears as he is assigned in the parish (Midden, 2016). He is usually left alone in the world and has no safety net to cope with things which are not sufficiently taught in the seminary. Seminary training does not normally provide much attention to handling love and physical attraction in the long years of priests' formation. "For the most part, priestly training involves morality—the dos and don'ts of priestly life. Mostly, as one might imagine, the don'ts" (Midden, 2016). With mandated celibacy, the newly-ordained priest usually finds himself alone or in the company of one or two co-pastors in a parish who are not personally close to him due to differences in seminary training, age, personality, or ecclesiastical status.

---

[1] Jayeel Serrano Cornelio, "Priesthood Satisfaction and the Challenges Priests Face: A Case Study of a Rural Diocese in the Philippines", *Religions* 2012, 3, 1111. https://doi.org/10.3390/rel304110, 1111.

Relative Autonomy of Priestly Life in the Parish

Loneliness does not mean solitude. Individuals can be lonely in front of many people if there is no intimacy and meaningful and intimate social interaction between them. In the case of diocesan priests, loneliness primarily consists of being isolated from their fellow priests and bishop. Being celibate, secular priests have no families. Most of the time, priests are alone in their parishes, especially if they are assigned in remote areas. Clerics are usually busy doing parish work, and administering the sacraments and sacramentals during Saturdays and Sundays. But on ordinary days, unless they hold other administrative or teaching jobs, priests are usually free to make their own schedule and itinerary. According to some informants, priests usually leave their parishes and follow their personal schedule after performing their assigned tasks, often without informing their superiors or parishioners of their whereabouts. Research on CSA indicated that sexual abuse usually occurs in situations where the predator priest is left alone with the victim either in the parish, victim's residence, or in some trips without the supervision of other people.

There is no pressure for diocesan priests to spend the rest of his time to other pastoral work, such as doing house-to-house pastoral visits with his parishioners or engage in other pastoral endeavors outside the parish pastoral plan. According to priests-informants, diocesan clerics have discretionary power to decide on how to spend his free time in the parish. Unlike in the seminary where formators are constantly monitoring the seminarians' behavior, the bishop and parishioners usually do not have no a monitoring system to track down the whereabouts of their priests in case they engage in CSA or other forms of deviant behavior in the diocese and parish. Without the obligatory practice of wearing the cassock after Vatican II, the public could not easily identify clerics from lay people when traveling outside their parishes or dioceses. The wearing of civilian clothes can provide anonymity and opportunity for priests to engage in deviant acts. Informants of this study agreed that the wearing of the cassock can somehow deters seminarians and priests to do immoral acts.

The scheduling of the priest's routine, especially his free time after Sunday liturgical services, can be crucial in preventing CSA. This is the problem with celibate priests, they have no families which can directly supervise their daily routine. Except for official functions, parish priests and their pastors are free to schedule their daily routine with absolute privacy. A routine activity approach has received a great deal of attention in recent years in the study of crime and delinquency. According to this approach, the opportunities that arise from routine and everyday life are crucial in explaining crime and deviant behavior. It emphasizes that crime is affected by the sociostructural patterning of people's routine activities. According to Cohen and Felson's (1979) original formulation, the rate of 'direct contact predatory crime" depends on the frequency of opportunities to commit such crimes, opportunities that people encounter in everyday situations. Thus, with anonymity, especially for clerics in the city, celibacy, and compete privacy can create deviant opportunities for clerics without the a systematic surveillance of superiors, families, and lay parishioners.

The rate of predatory crime such as CSA depends on the frequency in which routine activities bring together a motivated offender, a suitable target, and the absence of a capable guardian. A pedophile priest, for instance, who is often alone with his altar boys in his own parish during weekdays, where there are fewer people in the parish and no communal activities in the presbyterium, is placed in a routine structure that facilitates sexual abuse. Likewise, a heterosexual priest in a remote parish who has lesser activities during weekdays and no brother priests to talk to except his attractive female secretary is in a routine structure which prone to clerical abuse. Most clerical abuses occur when the offender is in complete control of the situation without effective guardians who can monitor or stop him in case he abuses minors, adolescents or adults under his care.

Unlike religious priests who are usually supported by their congregations and sent to remote areas with a strong missionary spirit to Christianize some natives or pagans with a feeling that they are men "on a mission", secular priests generally feel that they are doing routinary work and continuing only what the religious missionaries had started in the past. The secular priest is usually assigned to an established parish which can support him, otherwise, the religious order which organizes it would not turn it over to the diocese. The lack of frequent interactions with and support from their fellow priests, who are usually busy with their respective priestly duties, is the unintended effect of the loose social structuring of the diocesan priesthood.

In general, there is no frequent personal encounter and meaningful interaction between bishops and their secular priests. There is also a lack of formal and informal social networks which can act as intermediaries between the bishops and their secular priests. There is no coercion on the part of the bishops to monitor or supervise regularly the daily life of their priests in the parishes. In some cases, long distances between parishes in a big diocese, especially in developing countries, can be a hindrance of the bishops' regular visitation of the parishes. Finally, there is also no systematic use of the latest communication technologies by bishops to track down the activities of their priests in the parishes. The website "Voice of the Faithful" aptly describes the relative autonomy of diocesan priests from their bishops:

> Although priests owe obedience to their bishop, in most of their daily activities they are relatively independent. Once a man is ordained, he receives very little supervision. He is not subject to performance appraisals, receives very little feedback from other priests—and certainly not from the faithful in any constructive manner—and is seldom monitored in his daily activities. This relative independence allowed some priests to commit deviant acts which are often unnoticed by their bishops and reported by the reluctant laity (Voice of the Faithful, 206, p. 5).

Unlike religious priests who tend to have a more cohesive social bonding in their religious orders or congregations with their frequent communal activities, diocesan priests are relatively independent in their priestly life with fewer opportunities for communal bonding with their fellow clerics. The only regular meeting or activity is usually the weekly presbyterium meeting of priests with their bishop. In one diocese, this is usually a communal gathering and a common lunch in the Cathedral rectory with the bishop. Before this lunch, they usually have informal conversations with their fellow priests. If there is an important issue or problem in the diocese, the bishop will usually call for a meeting before the communal meal. But there seems to be no intimate sharing of clerical problems and concerns among the participants during this weekly gathering as one interviewee of the study of Jayeel Serrano Cornelio (2012) aptly described the overall atmosphere of this meeting: "There's the Monday gathering but priests are typically there to chat over a beer. Sometimes, I think to myself that I'm willing to share my condition, but no one asks anyway."[2]

The Bishops' Role in Clerical Behavior

The role of bishops in fostering a strong sense of clerical community with his diocesan priests is crucial in preventing CSA. A bishop is a spiritual father to his priests and a unifying factor to the clerical community in the diocese called the presbyterium. But the relationship and intimacy of the bishop with his priests in actual social practice is usually far from what the decree *Presbyterorum Ordinis* says concerning the relationship of priests with their bishops, which emphasizes the communion of the local clergy under one priesthood[3]:

> All priests, in union with bishops, so share in one and the same priesthood and ministry of Christ that the very unity of their consecration and mission requires their hierarchical communion with the order of bishops. (32) At times in an excellent manner, they manifest this communion in liturgical concelebration as joined with the bishop when they celebrate the Eucharistic Sacrifice. (33) Therefore, by reason of the gift of the Holy Spirit which is given to priests in Holy Orders, bishops regard them as necessary helpers and counselors in the ministry and in their role of teaching, sanctifying and nourishing the People of God. (34)[4]

This decree also indirectly requires the bishop to provide sufficient material and spiritual support to his priests and to create a system which takes care of the personal and spiritual needs of his brother priests to achieve the pastoral goals of the diocese. It gives him three main obligations to his priests, namely: to be concerned with their material and spiritual well-being; to provide them with a continual formation; and to listen and engage in dialogue with them on the necessities of pastoral work and welfare of the diocese:

> Bishops should always embrace priests with a special love since the latter to the best of their ability assume the bishops' anxieties and carry them on day by day so zealously. They should regard the priests as sons and friends (13) and be ready to listen to them. Through

---

[2]Jayeel Serrano Cornelio, "Priesthood Satisfaction and the Challenges Priests Face: A Case Study of a Rural Diocese in the Philippines," *Religions* 2012, 3, 1111. https://doi.org/10.3390/rel304110, 1111.

[3]Chap. 2, Sections "The Composition of the Catholic Hierarchy", "The Interaction Between Bishops, the Roman Curia, and the Pope"

[4]See Presbyterorum Ordinis, Chap. 2, Section "The Composition of the Catholic Hierarchy", Retrieved 18 May 2017, http://www.vatican.va/archive/hist_councils/ii_vatican_council/documents/vat-ii_decree_19651207_presbyterorum-ordinis_en.html.

their trusting familiarity with their priests they should strive to promote the whole pastoral work of the entire diocese.[5]

The enforcement of the directives of this decree, however, becomes problematic. With the lack of intermediary authority participated by the laity that directly monitors and pressures diocesan bishops to enforce these directives in the diocesan or district level, the implementation would be difficult. It is recognized in sociolegal studies, following the Weberian definition of law, that an important element of effective law enforcement is psychological coercion, a psychological fear for the subjects of the law that they would surely be punished if they violate the legal provisions. On paper, the text is ideal to address the many personal and pastoral needs of the priests. In actual social practice, enforcement is problematic as there is no effective enforcing agency in the diocesan level to systematically enforce this Church's decree.

All dioceses of the RCC under the resident bishops usually do not have committees which are managed by experts who proactively help priests to identify and respond to their social and psychological needs. According to key informants, it is usually the priest with a serious psychological problem who will approach the bishop, who, in turn, would send him to a psychological center to assist him. At this stage, the problem could have already gone serious since no intervening group which proactively monitors clerical problems. In cases of CSA, the erring priest usually hides his deeds from his bishop. Thus, the abuse could first escalate and develop into a scandal before the problem could be discovered by the bishop.

In general, secular priests enjoy relative independence from their bishops in managing their parishes. But this relative distance between priests and their bishops also often results in little support for financial, pastoral, and personal needs in the parish, especially in poorer dioceses. The priest-respondents in the study of Cornelio (2012) in one rural diocese on priesthood satisfaction, for instance, complained that they felt being neglected by diocesan leaders, the bishop included, with regard to their pastoral and personal needs. The study also showed a pattern that when priests do not feel being listened to by the institutional leaders, they tend to distance themselves and eventually become distrusting of their bishops. This is also the sentiment of some priests-informants of this study who complained that there are instances that their archbishop who took over as the new administrator, after the resident bishop died, did not consult them regarding his new policy that provided a lower and uniform allowances for all priests in the diocese, regardless if one is assigned in a small or big parish.

Due to lack of frequent communal activities for strong social bonding, diocesan priests tend to live independent lives—except of course, when their co-pastors where they are assigned happened to be their seminary friends—and manage their parish with greater autonomy from their bishops. If parish priests have close ties with their bishops because of friendship, ethnicity, kinship, seniority, or other considerations, and their parish pastoral councils are subservient to them, they can actually run their

---

[5]*Christum Dominus*: Decree Concerning Pastoral Office of Bishops in the Church, Retrieved 13 May 2017, http://www.vatican.va/archive/hist_councils/ii_vatican_council/documents/vat-ii_decree_19651028_christus-dominus_en.html.

parishes with more discretionary powers similar to the relative autonomy enjoyed by their bishops in the diocesan level of the RCC.

Unless restricted by their bishops, parish priests have total control over the daily operation of the parishes. The relative independence of diocesan priests in the parish came out in some court proceedings on CSA. Church officials, for instance, often use, as a court defense, the autonomy of the parish and secular priests. This is quite reflective of the real situation in the parish level where diocesan priests have weak social bonding. There is some grain of truth of this defense by some Church officials when they denied responsibility in a rape case filed by an alleged victim of a dead priest in the New South Wales Hunter Valley. Church representatives denied the complete supervision of bishops over their diocesan priests as it fought a claim for civil damages in court. Although under the command responsibility principle, it is debatable to believe that bishops have no responsibility and supervision over their clergy within their jurisdictions. But the real situation in the parish generally shows that secular priests, indeed, enjoy a greater degree of autonomy under the CCL. The diocesan bishop could not then be fully responsible then for their actions.[6]

This admission that diocesan priests enjoy certain independence in the parishes and that bishops do not normally interfere in their clerical life is an indication that priests do not have a cohesive community under the leadership of their bishops which can inhibit clerical abuse. The bishops can be a distant authority figure for their priests. They do not normally intervene in their parish life except when there are serious cases of doctrinal violations or CSA. They do not usually reach out to their priests and monitor their behavior on a regular basis to prevent CSA. There is no strong bonding among secular priests either, supported by a strong social structure which monitors clerical abuse.

Meet and Greet for Diocesan Priests with their Bishops

The personal consultation between the bishop and his priest is usually occasional, although there can be a weekly encounter during the presbyterium assembly. Except for urgent matters, priests do not usually see bishops for consultation on personal matters. According to informants in one diocese, priests can often see their bishop in the weekly presbyterium meeting in the Cathedral. If there is no official agenda set by the bishop or his vicar for discussion and decision, this meeting usually function as an informal get-together for priests in the diocese. They also mentioned that this

---

[6]Giselle Wakatama, "Catholic Church officials deny responsibility for supervising priests as it faces damages lawsuit", (11 April 2017), Retrieved 18 May 2017, http://www.abc.net.au/news/2016-02-10/catholic-church-officials-deny-responsibility/7152604.

weekly meeting is not compulsory. There is no sanction if some priests could not attend this gathering. Moreover, the meeting is not structured in a way that there is a meaningful interaction and sharing of personal and pastoral problems among priests in the diocese. In general, priests only interact with their friends and former classmates in the seminary during this encounter.

Except for the yearly retreat and some monthly recollections—some diocesan priests may even skip these spiritual activities without grave sanctions according to some informants—there is no systematic spiritual formation for priests similar to seminary training. There is a diocesan curia which assists the bishop in managing the diocese. But it seemed to be functioning only when there is a serious issue that involves some members of the diocesan clergy. Besides, the convening of the diocesan curia usually depends on the bishop. With the bishop's plenary powers on matters of the priesthood and church administration, he is still the ultimate decision-maker in the diocese and can ignore the advice or suggestions of his curia, presbyterium, or lay associations in the diocese. For instance, in one diocese, according to key informants, the bishop was reminded by the presbyterium that the land titles of some Church's real properties under his name be transferred to the diocese, but he never did as he promised. Diocesan lawyers even presented to him legal documents for him to sign to transfer the properties to the diocese during his dying moments, but according to informants, he continued to refuse until his demise. This case only illustrates the vast discretionary powers of the bishop which could hardly be overruled by anyone in the diocese except the pope. Under Canon 381,1 of the CCL, a diocesan bishop has all the ordinary, proper, and immediate power which is required for the exercise of his pastoral function in the diocese.[7]

Because of the injunction of *Ordinis Presbyterorum* to maintain the unity and communion of the clergy, it is only the bishop who has the direct supervision of his priests as the father of the diocese. But in actual social practice, it seems that the bishop can only act as an authority figure to priests but not as a compassionate "father" and "friend" as described by the decree. He can be a distant observer to his priests, especially if he has no strong friendship and frequent social interaction with his priests. In a big diocese with a large number of priests, supervision of the daily affairs of the parish is not usually done by local ordinaries. The bishop does not normally visit his priests regularly unless there is an urgent pastoral problem or there is a significant activity or anniversary in the parish.

The Social Interaction among Bishops

One important venue where bishops can meet and improve their interpersonal relationship within a region or country is the episcopal conference or the bishops' conference. The concept of forming episcopal conferences started in 1965 with Second

---

[7]See Article 2 Diocesan Bishops, *Code of Canon Law.* Retrieved 18 May 2017, http://www.vatican.va/archive/ENG1104/_P1E.HTM.

Vatican Council (Vatican II) which issued a decree called *Christus Dominus* or the Decree on the Pastoral Office of Bishops in the Church. In paragraph 38, it defined a bishops' conference as:

> An episcopal conference is a form of assembly in which the bishops of a certain country or region exercise their pastoral office jointly in order to enhance the Church's beneficial influence on all men, especially by devising forms of the apostolate and apostolic methods suitably adapted to the circumstances of the times (*Christus Dominus*, 38).[8]

An episcopal conference can be either be regional or national. A regional conference is a voluntary organization of bishops, recognized by the Congregation of Bishops in Rome, which consists of various national conferences but located in the same geographical region. It functions as a coordinating body between episcopal conferences and bishops residing within the region. A national bishops' conference is an assembly of bishops within one country or ecclesiastical territory which is formally recognized by the Roman Curia. The membership of in this organization is compulsory, although bishops retain their powers and authority in their dioceses.

The primary occasion for the personal encounter among bishops is when they meet in regional and national bishops' conferences. The Sacred Congregation of Bishops of the Roman Curia is in-charge of creating and supervising bishops' conferences. Regional bishops conferences are however voluntary associations. Bishops under their jurisdictions can opt not to join them. The Federation of Asian Bishops, for instance, describes itself as "a voluntary association of episcopal conferences in South, Southeast, East and Central Asia, established with the approval of the Holy See. Its purpose is to foster among its members solidarity and co-responsibility for the welfare of the Church and society in Asia, and to promote and defend whatever is for the greater good" (FABC Website). FABC functions through a hierarchy of structure consisting of the Plenary Assembly, the Central Committee, the Standing Committee, and the Central Secretariat. Its functions are primarily related to the promotion of the Church's apostolate in the light of Vatican II, common pastoral problems, coordination, service to episcopal conferences, as well as fostering development and inter-religious dialogue within the region. Although they increase the social interaction of bishops in a certain region, regional bishops' conferences are pastoral or work-oriented associations and have no comprehensive programs to intensify the personal bonding of the clergy in the regions.

The Interaction Between Bishops, the Roman Curia, and the Pope

The problem with bureaucratization of a large institution like the RCC is social alienation and a weakening of personal ties. The unintended effect of a growing institution is the loss of personal intimacy and anonymity. The Catholic Church

---

[8]Bishop Robert F. Basa, "The Bishop and the Conference", Catholic Culture.Org., Retrieved 26 2017, https://www.catholicculture.org/culture/library/view.cfm?recnum=9417.

started with a small group of apostles with Christ as their leader. But after more than 2,000 years in existence, the group has grown into a worldwide religious organization with 1.27 billion or 17.8% of the global population as of 2014.[9] And the number of bishops worldwide has already reached 5,237 in 2014 compared to 4,841 a year earlier. The total number of priests—diocesan and religious—around the world also increased to 415,792.[10] The Church claims that the clergy or the CH is a community of clerics who participate in the priesthood of Christ. Is this claim supported by an opportunity structure which promotes clerical solidarity and mutual support?

Ad Limina Apostolorum *Visits*

According to the CCL (Canon 400), "a bishop is bound to make a report to the Supreme Pontiff on the state of the diocese entrusted to him" every five years and this report should be made in conjunction with the *ad limina apostolorum* visit:

> Every five years the diocesan Bishop is bound to submit to the Supreme Pontiff a report on the state of the diocese entrusted to him, in the form and at the time determined by the Apostolic See (Canon 399,1).

Ad limina Apostolorum visit—or "to the threshold of the Apostles" visit refers to the pilgrimage to the tombs of Saints Peter and Paul in Rome that all bishops are required to make:

> Unless the Apostolic See has decided otherwise, in the year in which he is bound to submit the report to the Supreme Pontiff, the diocesan Bishop is to go to Rome to venerate the tombs of the Blessed Apostles Peter and Paul, and to present himself to the Roman Pontiff (Canon 400,1).

Owing to the growing number of dioceses, most *ad limina* visits now occur every eight or nine years. With more than 2,850 dioceses worldwide, a pope would have to meet more than 570 bishops each year to hit the five-year target. A one-on-one encounter between the bishop and the Pope would not be possible. Thus, the retired Pope Benedict XVI began the practice of holding more informal meetings with groups of bishops on *ad limina* instead of individual meetings. Pope Francis has continued this practice, although, like Pope Benedict, he also tried to grant the requests of individual bishops who feel a need for a private meeting (CNS News, 20 Dec 2016).

---

[9] Estimated by "Annuario Pontificio 2016," the Vatican yearbook as cited in Junno Arocho Esteves, "Vatican statistics report increase of baptized Catholics worldwide", *National Catholic Reporter*, Retrieved 8 May 2017, https://www.ncronline.org/news/vatican/vatican-statistics-report-increase-baptized-catholics-worldwide.

[10] As estimated by "Annuario Pontificio 2016," the Vatican yearbook as cited in Junno Arocho Esteves, "Vatican statistics report increase of baptized Catholics worldwide", *National Catholic Reporter*, Retrieved 8 May 2017, https://www.ncronline.org/news/vatican/vatican-statistics-report-increase-baptized-catholics-worldwide.

At present, *ad limina* visits are usually done as the bishops' pilgrimage for an audience with the pope, meetings with senior members of the Roman Curia, and visits to a number of holy sites. With eight to nine years interval, *ad limina* visits could not possibly foster personal intimacy with the Pope, fellow bishops, and Roman Curia. They could not also provide the Pope an in-depth understanding of the bishops' daily administration of their respective dioceses. The group *ad limina* could not provide the bishops with some quality time with the Pope on personal matters.

The primary goal of the "ad limina" visit is to foster collegiality between the bishops and the pope and "an exchange of faith and Christian witnessing". It is also an opportunity for the bishops from neighboring dioceses to make a pilgrimage together; the visits consists of obligatory prayer at the tombs of St. Peter and St. Paul and celebration of Masses in the major basilicas of Rome and other prayer opportunities. Together with this personal encounter with the Pope is the submission of a report by every bishop to the Roman Curia on the status of the diocese. A segment of this report usually deals with vocation promotions and seminaries, which will be forwarded in advance to the Congregation for the Clergy, giving the visiting bishop and congregation officials a chance to discuss issues of specific concern (CNS News, 20 Dec 2016).

Ad limina visit, which is done once every five years, and sometimes suspended if the Pope is busy, could not therefore foster a strong bonding between the Pope and the bishops.[11] Although its primary purpose is to foster brotherhood and collegiality, *Ad limina* visit could hardly enhance the social bonding between the bishops, the pope and clerical officials of the Roman Curia.

Interaction in Councils and Synods

Other occasions of clerical interaction in the CH are the general councils and the synods of bishops in the RCC. Universal councils are only occasional legislative gatherings in the Church. They are usually convened by popes when there are serious doctrinal and pastoral matters that affect the universal church. The last universal council convened by the Pope is the Second Vatican Council which was held in Rome from 1962 to 1965. Since then the pope has no plans yet to convene this kind of council in the near future to further enhance the universal brotherhood of the CH as a clerical community, aside from producing new decrees and teachings for the universal Church. The main objective of this gathering is to address the doctrinal and pastoral needs of the Church and not just to promote the interpersonal relationships of all bishops in the world with the pope as the overall head. Albeit bishops get to know each other during session breaks, a universal council is primarily a formal gathering and not a team building encounter.

The Synod of Bishops is also another occasion which can provide an opportunity for the pope and bishops to meet and interact together as members of the CH. The CCL defines the synod of bishops as:

---

[11]Pope Frances, for instance, suspended the *Ad Limina* visits of bishops to celebrate the Year of Mercy in 2016 (CNS News, 20 Dec 2016).

a group of bishops who have been chosen from different regions of the world and meet together at fixed times to foster closer unity between the Roman Pontiff and bishops, to assist the Roman Pontiff with their counsel in the preservation and growth of faith and morals and in the observance and strengthening of ecclesiastical discipline, and to consider questions pertaining to the activity of the Church in the world (Canon 342).

The Synod of Bishops is a permanent institution established by Pope Paul VI in 1965 to respond to the desire of the bishops at Vatican II to keep alive the positive spirit engendered by the experience of the council. The word "synod", derived from two Greek words *syn*, meaning "together", and *hodos*, meaning "road" or "way". Literally, it means a "coming together". A Synod is therefore a religious meeting or assembly at which bishops, gathered around and with the Pope, have the opportunity to interact with each other and to share wisdom, information, and experiences, in the common pursuit of pastoral solutions which have universal validity and application.

John Paul II called the synod as "a means or instrument of the collegiality of bishops"[12]. The synods of bishops can either be "ordinary", which are scheduled at fixed intervals, or "extraordinary", which are convened only to address some important matter. The participants are usually fewer, consisting of the heads of Eastern Catholic Churches, the presidents (only) of episcopal conferences, three members of religious institutes and the cardinals who head dicasteries of the Roman Curia.

As of October 2014, there have been three such assemblies, in 1969, 1985, and 2014.[13] The synod of bishops may foster a more intimate encounter than the universal council. But its bonding effect is usually minimal as it usually consists of a few bishops who represent the universal church in the meeting. Besides, its focus is more on doctrinal and pastoral issues rather than promoting social interaction and intimacy among bishops.

Papal Pastoral Visits

Finally, pastoral visits of the pope to a specific country or region are also occasions for social bonding for bishops and priests with the Supreme Pontiff. But these visits are occasional. The itinerary is set in advance to places which usually need an urgent pastoral response by the Pope. Again, the primary objective is apostolic in nature and not just to meet the bishops and the local clergy in intimate dialogue to understand their personal concerns. This papal visit is also an opportunity for the pope to visit the local churches and meet the local bishops and the clergy as a clerical community. But this encounter can hardly result in an intimate social bonding between diocesan priests, bishops, and the pope. When Pope Francis visited the Philippines, for

---

[12] Speech to the Council of the Secretariat of the Synod of Bishops, 30 April 1983: *L'Osservatore Romano*, 1 May 1983.

[13] Irish Catholic Bishops' Conference, "The Synod of Bishops in Rome—Frequently Asked Questions", Retrieved 15 may 2017, http://www.catholicbishops.ie/2015/09/29/archbishops-eamon-martin-diarmuid-martin-attend-synod-bishops-rome/.

instance, it was reported in the media that the some members of the diocesan clergy took a lot of selfies and pictures with him instead of spending more quality time with him, personally talking to him their personal problems and concerns.

Spiritual Network and Social Bonding in the Clerical Community

An intense group solidarity among the clergy can provide numerous benefits to individual bishops and secular priests, such as emotional support and a strong sense of brotherhood. A highly networked social interaction and spiritual formation are necessary to increase the social network and social control of all the members of the CH. Unlike non-religious communities, the clerical community has an additional social control mechanism which checks clerical misconduct such as CSA—the inner or spiritual social control. This means that as spiritual ministers their spirituality must be more intense than that of the ordinary believers to make them credible role models and preachers. But this requires a more stable and efficient structure of spiritual formation for the clergy.

Spirituality has two dimensions: individual or private religiosity, expressed in terms of prayer and individual devotions, and the public religiosity, expressed in terms of public rituals and common spiritual activities. The "atomistic" structure of the secular clergy, where dioceses are relatively autonomous from one another, just as bishops and diocesan priests are relatively independent in their own jurisdictions, is a primary hurdle to social cohesion and mutual support. This is reinforced by the vast discretionary powers of the local bishops in handling the local affairs of the RCC. The Supreme Pontiff and Cardinals of the Roman Curia in Rome are distant authority figures who usually intervene only on serious ecclesiastical matters, particularly on heresy or incorrect interpretation of the Church's doctrines and grave abuses by bishops or priests, but rarely in ordinary diocesan affairs.

There are two important dimensions which can enhance the social bonding of the clergy and inhibit deviance: the common spiritual activities and frequent personal interactions of clerics in the CH either within the diocese or episcopal conference. The peculiarity of the CH as a community is that it is not merely a human group bonded by common secular interests but also a religious community that seeks to commune with Christ as their ultimate religious leader. Thus, it does not only seek social bonding but also spiritual intimacy with him through constant prayer and strong communal spirituality. CH sees itself as a human community "marching" towards beatific vision with God in the next life.

The Church doctrine teaches the three types of ecclesial communities which form a unity: the Church militant here on earth, the Church in suffering in purgatory, and the Church in glory in heaven (CCC, 954). The decree *Prebytorum Ordininis* enjoins all bishops, led by the pope and the Roman Curia, to promote clerical social bonding and spiritual formation of the clergy, and for pastors to undergo an ongoing purification of sins while journeying towards the Church in glory. An intense spiritual bonding of the clergy with God and fellow priests can provide a strong internal control against deviance, even if the clergy may has a lesser opportunity for social interaction.

Nurturing the spirituality of the clergy to prevent CSA in the RCC lacks the necessary social structure. Aside from the yearly retreat and occasional communal spiritual activities, there is no holistic, universal uniform, and sustainable spiritual formation for all the secular clergy in the RCC. Unlike religious priests who are closely connected with their religious orders or congregations through a more structured religious formation, the diocesan bishops and priests, including the pope and cardinals of the Roman Curia relatively autonomous life with no systematic program to enhance their private and public spirituality. The papacy is even considered as one of the loneliest jobs in the RCC. The administrators of the Roman Curia, unless they belong to religious orders, usually live in independent apartments or residences with minimal communal activities and prayers.

There is a lack of intermediary lay and clerical supervisory bodies which regularly visit the dioceses around the world and cross-connect them and, if necessary, impose effective sanctions, to ensure that the diocesan clergy is given adequate spiritual formation. There are two important sacred congregations of the Roman Curia which oversee the bishops and the clergy: Sacred Congregation of the Clergy and the Sacred Congregation of the Bishops. But these administrative bodies are loaded with ecclesiastical responsibilities resulting in less time, personnel, and resources to visit and monitor thousands of dioceses and clergy around the world. Moreover, the RCC is slow in tapping the latest technologies to supervise clerical behavior, often leaving it to the priests' individual consciences and discretion of the bishops to discipline negligent priests in their spiritual life. A strong individual and collective spirituality is an important component of the direct social control which can prevent CSA. Unfortunately, this ideal is not firmly supported by the Church's social structure.

Diocesan priests are practically left on their own as to how, when, and where to practice private spirituality. Unlike in religious orders or seminaries, clerics in active ministry in the parish do not have a system as to some sort of on how and when to do their individual prayers and acts of devotion. Seminarians usually have regular consultations with their spiritual directors on how to enhance their individual spirituality. But this set-up is not usually available in the ministry. It largely depends on the bishops' initiative to require their priests to intensify their private spirituality. But bishops rarely interfere in their priests' private religiosity. Priests, such as parish priests, have discretion on how often they would consult their spiritual directors if any, and how they would develop their own private devotions.

The public aspect of the religiosity of the clergy consists mainly of common spiritual rituals and activities, such as the annual retreats, group celebrations of the sacraments, and other religious activities. There is no clear and holistic program which promotes the ongoing spiritual formation of diocesan clergy. Each diocese has its own program for the enhancement of clerical spirituality. The pope and the

Roman Curia or the episcopal conference can provide guidelines for the continuous spiritual formation of diocesan clergy. But the implementation of these guidelines would largely depend on the local bishops who have the full control of their dioceses.

Summary

This chapter has shown that despite the assertion of the official Church that the members of the CH are united and in communion with one another under the leadership of the pope, the opportunity structure, however, of the social interaction and spiritual bonding of diocesan clerics in the various levels of the CH remains loose and lack of common activities and social interactions which can foster stronger social ties among the clergy which can inhibit CSA. The analysis has revealed that there are no strong intermediary networks participated by lay Catholics to connect and interconnect the various levels of the clerical social networks of the CH. The spiritual formation and social networks of clerics also remain problematic as there is no uniform and stable structure for the holistic spiritual formation and social bonding for all pastors in the RCC. All these factors point to a loosely knit communal structure of the CH that is prone to social disorganization and CSA.

References

Bellair, P. E. (1997). Social interaction and family crime: Examining the importance of neighbor networks. *Criminology, 35,* 667–704.
Boxenbaum, E., & Jonsson, S. (2008). Isomorphism, diffusion, and decoupling. In R. Greenwood, C. Oliver, R. Suddaby, & K. Sahlin-Anderson (Eds.), The Sage handbook of organizational institutionalism (pp. 78–98). Thousand Oaks, CA: Sage Publications.
Bursik, R. J. (1988). Social disorganization and theories of crime and delinquency: Problems and prospects. *Criminology, 26,* 519–51.
Clancy, R. (2008). *The perceptions of the recently ordained priests of boston of their post secondary education and formation in seminary.* PhD thesis, Boston College.
Cohen, L., & Felson, M. (1979). Social change and crime rate trends: A routine activities approach. *American Sociological Review, 44,* 588–607.
Cornelio, J. S. (2012). Priesthood satisfaction and the challenges priests face: A case study of a rural diocese in the philippines. *Religions, 3,* 1103–1119.
Formicola, J. R. (2016). The politics of clerical sexual abuse. *Religions, 7*(1), 9.
Granovetter, M. S. (1982). The strength of weak ties: A network theory revisited. In P. V. Mardsen & N. Lin (Eds.), *Social structure and network analysis* (pp. 105–130). Thousand Oaks, CA: Sage Publications.
Greenberg, S., W., Rohe, W. M., & Williams, J. R. (1982). *Safe and secure neighborhoods: Physical characteristics and informal territorial control in high and jaw crime neighborhoods.* Washington, D.C.: National Institute of Justice.
Hirschi, T. (1969). *Causes of Delinquency.* Berkeley, California: University of California Press.
Hawdon, J., & Ryan, J. (2009). Social capital, social control, and changes in victimization rates. *Crime & Delinquency, 55,* 526–549.

Kapsis, R. E. (1976). Continuities in delinquency and riot patterns in black residential areas. *Social Problems, 23,* 567–580.

Kapsis, R. E. (1978). Residential succession and delinquency. *Criminology, 15,* 459–486.

Kennedy, B. P., Kawachi, I., Prothrow-Stith, D., Lochner, K., & Gupta, V. (1998). Social capital, income inequality, and firearm violent crime. *Social Science and Medicine, 47,* 7–17.

Kornhauser, R. (1978). *Social Sources of Delinquency: An Appraisal of Analytic Models.* Chicago, IL: University of Chicago Press.

Kruger, D. J., Hutchison, P., Monroe, M. G., Reischl, T., & Morrel-Samuels, S. (2007). Assault injury rates, social capital, and fear of neighborhood crime. *Journal of Community Psychology, 35,* 483–498.

Midden, P. (2016). I've spent 30 years counseling priests who fall in love. Here's.

Moore, M. D., & Recker, N. (2013). Social capital, type of crime, and social control. *Journal of Research in Crime and Delinquency, 62*(6). https://doi.org/10.1177/0011128713510082.

Putnam, R. (2000). *Bowling alone: The collapse and revival of American community.* New York, NY: Simon & Schuster.

Rosenfeld, R., Messner, S. F., & Baumer, E. P. (2001). Social capital and homicide. *Social Forces, 80,* 283–310.

Schuth, K. (2016). *Seminary formation: Recent history-current circumstances-new directions.* Liturgical Press: Collegeville, MN: Liturgical Press.

Shaw, C., & McKay, H. (1942). *Juvenile delinquency and urban areas.* Chicago: Chicago University Press.

Thomas, W. I., & Znaniecki, F. (1958). *The Polish peasant in Europe and America.* New York, NY: Dover.

Zech, C., & Gautier, M. L. (2004). Catholic parish organizational structure and parish outcomes. *Journal for the Scientific Study of Religion, 43*(1), 141–150.

Chapter 3
Supervision of Clerical Behavior in the Hierarchy

Abstract The Catholic Church prides itself on having a united community of ordained pastors under one priesthood of Christ. This chapter attempts to analyze broadly this social cohesion of the Catholic hierarchy as a clerical community. It investigates the supervision and coordination of the various components of the hierarchical community from the pope and the Roman Curia down to the lowest clerical network of the parish and draws some implications to the social control of clerical behavior against sexual abuse. It argues that the weak social bonding of various networks within the hierarchy, the concentration of ecclesiastical powers in the college of bishops as a clerical network, the absence of a professional judicial system in the Church, the lack of technological surveillance against clerical abuse, and the inadequate lay intermediary networks in the hierarchy primarily contribute to the social disorganization of the Catholic clergy as a community.

Introduction

The social disorganization theory (SDT) hypothesizes that socially-organized communities exercise strong social control to keep criminal behavior in check, while the disorganized ones have weak, broken, or ineffective social monitoring of criminal behavior.[1] Social disorganization is understood as "the inability of a community to realize common goals and solve chronic problems" (Kornhauser, 1978). The SDT reemerged in the mid-1980s as one of the major theoretical perspectives in the study of crime. Originally developing out of the work of the early Chicagoans (Shaw and McKay, 1942), the theory focuses on the ecological (especially neighborhood) distribution of crime and delinquency, hypothesizing that it is due to the variation in the capacity of neighborhoods to constrain its residents from violating norms (Markowitz et al., 2000).

---

[1] Ronald L. Akers, *Social Learning and Social Structure: A General Theory of Crime and Deviance*: A General Theory of Crimes and Deviance. New Brunswick (USA) and London (UK): Transaction Publishers.

Contemporary work extends SDT and research in various directions (Markovitz et al., 2001): studying the role of unexpected change in the neighborhood; explicating the mediating role of cohesion, efficacy, and social ties in the causal process; examining the role of social disorder; and investigating demographic characteristics that condition the effect of cohesion on crime (Bellair, 1997, 2000; Bursik & Webb, 1982; Rountree & Warner, 1999; Sampson & Groves, 1989; Sampson & Raundenbush, 1999; Sampson et al., 1997; and Skogan, 1990; Warner & Rountree, 1997).

One significant intervening construct of the SDT is Shaw and McKay's (1942) theoretical model which sees the ability of the community to supervise groups within the community as crucial to preventing social disorganization and crime. The capacity of the community to control group-level dynamics is a key mechanism linking community dynamics with delinquency. This implies that a community which has a higher level of social control over their different groups is more likely to control deviant behavior than the one with low supervision due to weak social control and loose social cohesion. The prevalence of unsupervised groups is one indicator of socially disorganized communities. All communities practice social control to regulate and enforce their norms. Innes (2003) understood social control broadly as an organized action intended to change people's behavior to inhibit deviance. The inability of the Catholic hierarchy (CH) to rein in clerical behavior and stop the widening clerical sexual abuse CSA in the Roman Catholic Church (RCC) suggests a weak social bonding and social control of the various clerical networks within the hierarchy of bishops and priests.

This chapter attempts to analyze the social control and supervision of clerical behavior within the Church's hierarchical structure, from the papacy and Roman Curia down to the parish level. It aims to assess how each level of authority and social network of the hierarchy exercises control of clerical behavior within the network and with other clerical networks to increase compliance with ecclesiastical norms on priestly behavior. The RCC observes the principles of solidarity and subsidiarity. The principle of solidarity observes the unity and interdependence of the different clerical networks within the hierarchy, while the principle of solidarity sees the coordination of the various levels of authority within the community; thus, if one level of authority does not function well for the good of the community, the affected network can appeal to a higher level of authority, or the higher network can intervene if it sees a malfunctioning in the lower level.

The SDT assumes that the prevalence of unsupervised and autonomous groups and networks within a community can weaken social control which can lead to the persistence of certain crimes and deviance. This book argues that the greater autonomy and weak supervision of the various levels of the Church hierarchy (CH) from the Roman Curia down to the parishes, the absence of professional judicial system in the Church, and most especially, the over-concentration of ecclesiastical powers around the social network of the bishops, are some of the major disorganizing factors that weaken the supervision and social control of clerical behavior against CSA in the CH.

Limited Supervisory Powers of the Roman Curia

A hierarchy consisting of a pope, bishops, priests, and deacons governs the RCC. Most organizations, especially nation-states, have hierarchical structures, most also have a balance of power, thus separating the executive, the legislative, and the judicial powers. In the RCC, the pope and the Vatican sacred congregations which directly report to him exercise all these three powers. Despite the Second Vatican Council's (Vatican II) emphasis on the collegiality of the bishops, Pope John Paul II and Pope Benedict XVI re-emphasized Rome's authority in the entire RCC.

The highest governing body of the RCC is the Roman Curia. The Roman Curia is the central government of the Church that assists the Pope in his universal governance and service to the people of God. The name "curia" is taken from the Latin word meaning "court," and just as every diocese and archdiocese has a chancery or diocesan curia, the Holy See also has a central staff. The "Curia began literally as the small papal court and evolved gradually over the centuries until 1588 when Pope Sixtus V gave it a formal organizational structure. The skeleton of offices and departments he created has remained up to the modern times, with many popes introducing various changes and reforms. Today, the Curia consists of secretariats, congregations (the main governing agencies), tribunals or judicial agencies, pontifical councils and committees, and several financial offices."[2]

The sacred congregations under the Roman Curia that directly supervise the bishops and priests are the Sacred Congregation of Bishops, the Sacred Congregation for the Doctrine of the Faith, and the Sacred Congregation of the Clergy. Each congregation has other duties aside from supervising bishops and priests. The supervision of these congregations has nothing to do with suppressing the powers of the bishops nor interfering directly with diocesan affairs, including the handling of clerical abuse except the Sacred Congregation for the Doctrine of the Faith which reviews CSA cases. The congregations of the Curia can only intervene with the explicit directive from the Pope. By its own authority, it cannot directly sanction bishops and their priests without the pope's authority. The bishops are higher in authority than the Congregation of Bishops in the Roman Curia. Only the pope can sanction bishops. Thus, the congregation cannot directly control and supervise local ordinaries. The Congregation for Clergy or the Sacred Congregation for the Doctrine of the Faith cannot also interfere with the bishops' decisions on clerical discipline in their diocesan affairs unless directly authorized by the pope. This creates a network dysfunction where a subordinate network consisting of bishops and their dioceses cannot be completely governed by the Roman Curia despite being higher in authority and the highest administrative body of the RCC.

In stressing how the universal Church subsists in the local Church, Vatican II has made it clear that the bishops should not be seen as agents of the Pope, let alone servants of the Curia, but that the Curia should be at the service of the College of Bishops. Although the Curia exists to give expression to the will of the Bishop of

---

[2]Matthew Bunson, "Understanding the Roman Curia An overview of the offices and leaders of the central government of the Catholic Church", Retrieved 13 May 2017, (17 May, 2015).

Rome, the Petrine ministry is not be a solitary one; as a classic formulation of the relationship between the pope and bishops, the first chapters of Acts declares: "Never Peter without the Eleven, never the Eleven without Peter." Vatican II's understanding of the governance of the RCC is known as "collegiality". This is also a key element of Pope Francis pontificate, and a mandate of the cardinals who elected him.[3]

Aside from the Curia, the regional and national bishops' conferences also exercise some supervision on the bishops and their priests. Despite the coordinating and supervisory role performed by bishops' conferences, the powers of the bishops within their dioceses remain intact. The CCL delimits the extent of the authority of the episcopal conference. Even the president of the conference cannot act in the name of all the bishops unless each and every bishop has given consent (Canon 455, 4). Thus, the conference cannot, on its own authority, cannot act in behalf of the member bishops. According to Canon 753, the local bishops remain the "authentic teachers and instructors of the faith for the faithful entrusted to their care in their dioceses."[4] So there is no for every bishop to attend all activities or obey the conferences' directives unless it is agreed by all members. Cardinal Ratzinger who became Pope Benedict IXVI reiterated the distinctive role of the bishop which cannot be interfered by episcopal conferences:

> Because it is a matter of safeguarding the very nature of the Catholic Church, which is based on an episcopal structure and not on a kind of federation of national churches. The national level is not an ecclesial dimension. It must once again become clear that in each diocese there is only one shepherd and teacher of the faith in communion with the other pastors and teachers and with the Vicar of Christ (The Ratzinger Report, 59–61).[5]

Vast Discretionary Powers of the Bishops

Although bishops owe allegiance and obedience to the pope, bishops live and manage their dioceses with relative independence and personally accountable only to the Pope for their actions and decisions. The 1983 CCL strengthened the power of the diocesan bishop on accountability. The strengthening of the role of the diocesan bishop, a key part of Vatican II, is well represented in the CCL. The bishop is not a delegate of the pope; he is the head of a particular church. Without weakening the pope's immediate and universal jurisdiction, this recognition empowers the diocesan bishop to carry out the threefold office of teaching, sanctifying, and shepherding while, at the same time, heightening his accountability (Alesandro, 2008).

Some documents of the RCC affirm the unity and collegiality of bishops. But the growing number of bishops and dioceses in the world makes it difficult for the

---

[3]Catholic Voices Comment, "Francis ushers in the age of collegiality" (3 May 2014), Retrieved 15 May 2017, https://cvcomment.org/2014/05/03/francis-brings-in-the-age-of-collegiality/.

[4]Bishop Robert F. Basa, "The Bishop and the Conference", Catholic Culture.Org., Retrieved 26 2017, https://www.catholicculture.org/culture/library/view.cfm?recnum=9417.

[5]Bishop Robert F. Basa, "The Bishop and the Conference", Catholic Culture.Org., Retrieved 26 2017, https://www.catholicculture.org/culture/library/view.cfm?recnum=9417.

pope and Roman Curia to constantly in contact with the CH in the daily affairs of the dioceses and supervise it to ensure that bishops strictly follow the Church's canon law and administrative guidelines. But the RCC has given bishops "absolute" ecclesiastical powers in dealing with the affairs of their dioceses:

> Individually, each bishop serves as the religious leader, financial head, and political connection to the secular world in which the Catholic Church operates. Religiously, the Bishop is charged with supervising all spiritual matters within his territorial purview, that is, his diocese. He is responsible for teaching, educating, and helping each individual to attain his/her spiritual fulfillment. All priests, nuns, and others who work for the diocese are under his management and control. As a financial leader, the Bishop serves as a "corporation sole" or as the individual who can sign contracts, carry out monetary matters and deal with civil, financial organizations in the name of the Church. The Bishop's diocese contains religious buildings, schools, hospitals, cemeteries and other real estate holdings which are considered, in a civil sense, as financial assets. As a political individual, the Bishop is often a liaison with civil authorities on policies that overlap both sacred and secular issues, especially those that impact education, health, and social services—indeed, a powerful individual to be consulted for co-operation on community needs.[6]

The bishop is usually assisted by College of Consultors, Diocesan Curia[7], Diocesan Commissions, and Diocesan Pastoral Council. The latter is not only composed of the laity but also clerics and religious. The canon lawyer Thomas P. Doyle believed that the CCL is a legal system in service to a monarchy. By its very nature, the primary goal is to protect the monarchs. This can be reflected in the giving of vast powers by the CCL to bishops who can act like monarchs in their dioceses liable only to the pope. There is no separation of powers in the RCC, hence no clear system of checks and balances, especially in the diocesan level.[8] In the absence of effective intermediary enforcement bodies between the bishops and the Roman Curia and the pope, the responsibility of disciplining and sanctioning erring priests lies heavily on the local bishop, archbishop or whoever heads the diocese or archdiocese. And with the doctrine of the Separation of Church and State, the state cannot even directly supervise and sanction the bishops of any wrongdoing or negligence in disciplining their priests, unless ecclesiastical laws that protect privacy and confidentiality of diocesan records and decisions of the bishops are amended.[9]

The CH prefers internal supervision concerning the discipline of the clergy. The RCC's response to CSA supports the belief that criminal abuse by clergy should be

---

[6]Jo Renee Formicola, "The Politics of Clerical Sexual Abuse", *Religions,* (2016), 5, Retrieved 15 May 2017, file:///C:/Users/Lenovo/Downloads/religions-07-00009.pdf.

[7]Canon 469 defines the diocesan curia as consisting of those institutions and persons which furnish assistance to the bishop in the governance of the entire diocese, especially in directing pastoral activity, in providing for the administration of the diocese and in exercising judicial power". The diocesan curia is composed of diocesan boards that advise the local bishops in managing the affairs of the diocese.

[8]Thomas P. Doyle, "Book offers insight into canon law's role in sexual abuse crisis", *The National Catholic Reporter, Apr. 22, 2015, Retrieved 24 May 2017,* https://www.ncronline.org/books/2015/04/book-offers-insight-canon-laws-role-sexual-abuse-crisis.

[9]This happened in the Boston and other parts of the United States, where statutes were changed to allow prosecutors of clerical sexual abuse to access diocesan records.

sanctioned by the Church internally—if at all—under the canonical commands of contrition and forgiveness, and not by civil authorities.[10] Bishops believe that their supervision of the clergy, even in sexual abuse situations, is an internal, supervisory matter to be handled by them, a traditional ecclesiastical right protected from state intrusion by historical, religious exemptions to civil law. Therefore, they relied either on the Church's legal system to adjudicate allegations of clerical sexual abuse or their own personal interpretations of Church laws to punish the priests under their control.[11]

Catholic bishops do not normally cooperate with the civil authority concerning CSA. In many cases, they would just transfer the abusive priests to other assignments within the diocese or send them abroad to avoid prosecution and scandal. Others would incardinate or transfer them to other dioceses, thus the civil authority loses jurisdiction over CSA cases with the change of territory. Some pedophile priests who were found guilty in American courts, for instance, were seen serving as missionaries in some Latin American countries. Pope Francis called this practice of "incardinating" or transferring abusive priests to other dioceses as "sickness of the times." He also warned the bishops of erring priests wandering or in transit from one place of another to act with "prudence and responsibility" in this area.[12]

The Holy See may be strict in enforcing the doctrines of the Church but not in enforcing administrative guidelines in the diocesan level. According to the Catholic teaching, only the bishop enjoys the fullness of the priesthood because he only can validly ordain priests and consecrate other bishops. Along with the right to ordain, the bishop has full monarchical authority over the local church. In a new Vatican training manual advising senior clergy on how to respond to allegations of abuse, it even states that only victims or their families should decide whether or not to report to authorities, although it said that bishops should be aware of local legal requirements.

> According to the state of civil laws of each country where reporting is obligatory, it is not necessarily the duty of the bishop to report suspects to authorities, the police or state prosecutors in the moment when they are made aware of crimes or sinful deeds[13]

The absolute powers of the bishops in their dioceses as well as the lack of intermediary networks such as lay councils to assist the bishops in dealing with CSA, is a disorganizing factor in the RCC. The failure of some bishops to do the right thing is a core element of the CSA crisis in the Church. Only the pope can really hold bishops accountable, leaving other clerical networks of the CH as well as the laity powerless to monitor and sanction clerical abuses by bishops in dealing with CSA cases such

---

[10]Wayne A. Logan, "Criminal Law Sanctuaries", *Harvard Civil Rights-Civil Liberties Law Review*, Vol 38, (2003), 321.

[11]Jo Renee Formicola, "The Politics of Clerical Sexual Abuse", *Religions,* (2016), 3, Retrieved 15 May 2017, file:///C:/Users/Lenovo/Downloads/religions-07-00009.pdf.

[12]Robert Mickens, "Catholic church needs better way to select bishops", National Catholic Reporter. Retrieved 8 May 2017, https://www.ncronline.org.

[13]Rachel Browne, "Vatican says Catholic bishops not compelled to report sex abuse", *The Sydney Morning Herald*, (11 Feb 206), Retrieved 10 May 2016, http://www.smh.com.au/national/vatican-says-catholic-bishops-not-compelled-to-report-sex-abuse-20160211-gmr6v7.html.

as cover-ups. And yet in court cases against CSA, the bishops appeared to be totally independent from the Holy See or the Roman Curia under the pope. There were efforts to sue the Vatican in American courts, for instance, over the CSA crisis which are premised on the notion that a bishop is an "employee" or an "official" of Rome. But Vatican lawyers emphasized the independence of local bishops. In a case filed in a U.S. district court in Kentucky, for instance, a Vatican attorney insisted that the Holy See does not exercise "day-to-day operational control" over bishops, and that bishops are more akin to independent contractors or franchisees than employees,[14] hinting that the college of bishops as a major clerical network of the CH is autonomous and beyond the control of the Roman Curia, papacy, and other social networks of the RCC.

Absence of Church's Judicial and Clerical Monitoring Systems

Another disorganizing factor for the CH in fighting CSA is the absence of a professional judicial system in the Church. The RCC has canon laws but it lacks professional tribunals, regional or national (and diocesan), if any, that can handle penal cases of priests such as CSA (Cafardi, 2008). Moreover, there are not enough canon lawyers, ecclesial prosecutors, and investigators to immediately handle CSA cases in the RCC. Thus, in the absence of judicial apparatuses and personnel such as those in the judiciary of the state which deal with criminal offenses, CSA cases could not be decided promptly and swiftly at the diocesan or local level. This situation can also delay the appeals of the accused to Rome for review. Without an efficient judicial system, the burden of deciding penal cases falls heavily on the bishops who are rarely canon lawyers and specialists in criminal court proceedings. The bishop becomes the sole judge and arbiter of justice of cases of CSA in his diocese. But with the absence of trained investigators and prosecutors to assist him, the objectivity of the facts of the case and the "rule of law" in the judicial process against abusive clerics can be in jeopardy. The verdict of the bishops can become subjective, depending on their level of friendship and connection between them and their accused priests as well as the perceived negative effects of the abuse cases to the image and unity of the Church. Most accusations against abusive clerics often end up in amicable settlements. Bishops often decide to privately pay civil damages and settle the cases out of court to avoid scandal.

Finally, the absence of a professional criminal justice system in the RCC can widen the discretionary powers of the bishops to handle cases of CSA. This discretion can cause delays which can encourage victims to bring the case to secular courts due to the inaction and perception of cover-ups by the local ordinary. It is established in

---

[14] John L. Allen, Jr., "The autonomy of bishops, and suing the Vatican". *National Catholic Reporter.* 21 May 2010, Retrieved 13 May 2017, https://www.ncronline.org/news/autonomy-bishops-and-suing-vatican.

law enforcement literature that the wide discretion of law enforcers can encourage abuse and rule-breaking behavior. With discretion, authorities who are tasked by law to sanction rule-breakers can instead encourage rule-breaking through intentional non-enforcement of law, by strategically taking no enforcement action, and through covert facilitation, that is, by taking hidden deceptive enforcement action, authorities intentionally encourage rule breaking (Marx, 1981).

The absence of a professional judicial system in the RCC and the over concentration of ecclesiastical powers in the network of the college of bishops, overpowering other supervisory networks such as the Roman Curia, papacy, and the laity, are two major disorganizing structures in the RCC which can tolerate cover-ups of CSA cases in the diocesan level.

Technology and Surveillance of Clerical Behavior

Technology's role in law enforcement historically has had a substantial effect on how enforcement officers complete their duties. Early technologies, such as the patrol vehicle, telephones, and two-way radios, were integral in the development of the modern law enforcement agency. The inclusion of evolving technology has developed and expanded the mission of law enforcement from solving crimes and answering calls for service to crime prevention (Wexler, 2012). The RCC, as a religious community which relies on trust, good conscience, and faith in God, does not depend much on modern technologies for surveillance of erring clergy and Church members who are involved in CSA. For this reason, it is the more necessary to empower lay intermediary agencies to monitor the clergy's actions and review bishops' decisions and investigations on CSA to avoid conspiracy and cover-up of abuse cases.

A holistic law or norm enforcement requires intermediary monitoring bodies, similar to civil society groups which supervise the state to fill the gaps in between levels of authority in society or large institution like the RCC. In the absence of these agencies and supervising networks, law enforcers could possess a wide range of discretion when and how to implement the law. This wide discretion of enforcers can lead to escalation, non-enforcement, and covert facilitation which can encourage rule-breaking behavior. The discretionary power of people who implement the norms has often been cited in criminology and sociology as a problem area in law enforcement. Gary Marx (1981), for instance, argues that illegality does not always stem from the absence of social control. On the contrary, situations exist where the presence of social control contributes to or even generates, criminal behavior. Law enforcers who have wide discretion can implement the substantive law different from the official one.

With vast powers of priests in their parishes and friendship ties with their bishops, victims of clerical abuse often encounter difficulties in bringing up their cases to Church authorities without independent ecclesiastical diocesan courts with competent canon lawyers and prosecutors. In the absence of independent ecclesiastical trial courts in a diocese ruled by an independent judge other than the local bishop where the victim can file a case against abusive priests, complaints by lay people on CSA would probably be ignored. In a Catholic country such as the Philippines, for instance, where the judiciary and justice department of the government are mostly managed by Catholics, some of which have friends in the clergy and are active in the Catholic religious organization in the parish, the probability of conviction in CSA cases would be low. A priest from one diocese in Mindanao, for instance, was accused of raping a young girl. The rape case was allegedly dismissed by the court, according to an informant close to the accused, because the Catholic governor of the province who is a benefactor of the priest and a close friend of the bishop, "intervened" in the case and used his influence over the judge to acquit the abusive cleric.[15]

Summary

This chapter has shown that the CH is as a community of clerics has different levels of authority and clerical networks. But the over-concentration of ecclesiastical authority in the network of the college of bishops has led to a disorganizing effect where other ecclesiastical networks such as the Roman Curia, the papacy, and the laity are weakened in supervisory powers to address CSA in the diocesan level. The primacy of the bishopric and monarchical powers of the bishops as well as the lack of intermediary lay networks, and technological surveillance against CSA has resulted in the relatively autonomous lives of clerics, accountable only to their bishops. Finally, the absence of a professional judicial system in the RCC with competent canon lawyers, prosecutors, and independent judges has led to vast disciplinary powers of the bishops in the dioceses against clerical abuse, giving them more discretionary powers to decide CSA cases in the RCC which can result in cover-ups and persistence of CSA.

References

Alesandro, J. (2008). The Code of Canon Law: Twenty-Five Years Later, Vol. 21 (USA, 2008).
Cafardi, N. (2008). *Before dallas: The bishops' response to the sexual abuse of children*. New Jersey: Paulist Press.
Bellair, P. E. (1997). Social interaction and community crime: examining the importance of neighbor networks. *Criminology, 35*(4), 677–703.
Bellair, P. E. (2000). Informal surveillance and street crime: a complex relationship. *Criminology, 38*(1),137–67.
Bursik, R. Jr., & Webb, J. (1982). Community Change and Patterns of Delinquency. *American Journal of Sociology, 88,* 24–42.
Innes, Martin. (2003). *Understanding social control: Deviance, crime and social order*. Maidenhead, UK: Open University Press.

---

[15]Based on a personal interview of the author with key informants in the local diocese. The accused is also a former co-seminarian of the author.

Kornhauser, R. (1978). *Social Sources of Delinquency: An Appraisal of Analytic Models*. Chicago, IL: University of Chicago Press. Note: The closing quotes must be before the citation, followed by a period.

Marx, G. T. (1981). Ironies of social control: Authorities as contributors to deviance through escalation, nonenforcement, and covert facilitation. *Social Problems, 28,* 221–246.

Markowitz, F. E., Bellair, P. E., Liska, A. E., & Liu, J. (2001). Extending social disorganization theory: Modeling the relationships between … *Criminology*; May 2001; 39, 2; Criminal Justice Periodicals pg. 293.

Sampson, R. J. & Groves, B. W. (1989). Community structure and crime: Testing Social Disorganization Theory. *American Journal of Sociology, 94,* 774–802.

Sampson, R. J. & Raudenbush, S. W. (1999). Systematic observation of public spaces: A new look at disorder in urban neighborhoods. *American Journal of Sociology, 105,* 603–651.

Sampson, R. J., Ruadenbush, S. W. & Earls, F. (1997). Neighborhoods and violent crimes: A multilevel study of collective efficacy. *Science, 277,* 918–924.

Skogan, W. G. (1990). *Disorder and Decline*. New York: Free Press.

Shaw, C. & McKay, H. (1942). *Juvenile Delinquency and Urban Areas*. Chicago: Chicago University Press.

Warner, B. & Rountree, P. (1997). Local social ties in a community and crime model: Questioning the nature of informal social control. *Social Problems, 44,* 520–536.

Wexler, C. (2012). *How are innovations in technology transforming policing?*. Washington, DC: Police Executive Research Forum.

Chapter 4
Celibacy and Social Disorganization in the Catholic Hierarchy

Abstract Using the social disorganization theory as the book's primary theoretical framework, this chapter discusses the crucial role of the family and married priesthood in the social control of clerical behavior and prevention of clerical sexual abuse in the Catholic Church's hierarchy. It draws on some research studies and secondary literature to stress the social disorganizing factor of the universal mandatory celibacy to the communal life of diocesan clerics against sexual abuse. It argues that the universal mandatory celibacy with its culture of clericalism deprives secular clergy of direct guardianship against clerical sexual abuse (CSA), given the lack of intimacy and social bonding among priests and between priests and their bishops in the dioceses and parishes. Living a celibate and relatively autonomous life, diocesan priests lack direct and indirect social controls offered by marital and family relations which can inhibit CSA. Social disorganization theory recognizes the crucial role of strong social bonding and social controls in preventing crime in organizations and communities.

Introduction

To become an ordained priest in the Roman Catholic Church (RCC) requires celibacy. Celibacy is a voluntary refusal to enter the married state, with total abstinence from sexual activity. It is defined as the withdrawal from reproduction, either voluntarily or under pressure, and is often associated with entry into a religious community (Abbott, 2001). In the RCC, those who receive ordination to become priests are obliged to profess the vow of celibacy.

Under Canon 277 of the Church's new Code of Canon Law (CCL), clerics are required to observe perfect and perpetual continence for the sake of the kingdom of heaven and, therefore, bound to practice celibacy. Its purpose is to make sacred ministers adhere more easily to Christ with an undivided heart and to dedicate themselves more freely to the service of God and humanity. Technically, diocesan priests profess the vow of celibacy—a promise not to marry, while members of religious orders take the vow of chastity. In essence, these two work the same way, and the terms can be used interchangeably.

© The Author(s), under exclusive license to Springer Nature Singapore Pte Ltd. 2019   61
V. O. Ballano, *Sociological Perspectives on Clerical Sexual Abuse in the Catholic Hierarchy*, SpringerBriefs in Religious Studies,
https://doi.org/10.1007/978-981-13-8825-5_4

The RCC's history has shown that being unmarried or celibate was not always an essential requirement for being a priest. "Evidence is abundant that mandatory celibacy was a late entry into Christianity, and did not exist in the second or third centuries. As a matter of fact, the Church today acknowledges that no law of celibacy as we know it today existed in the beginning" (Daniel, 2012). It took the RCC a thousand years before it requires the clergy to take the vow of celibacy.

Jesus himself recommends optional celibacy (Matthew 19:3–12). During the early years of Christianity, celibacy was only a voluntary ascetic practice of early Christian monks and some clerics, but not universally required for Catholic priests. It was only after the Church's Second Lateran Council in 1339 that mandatory celibacy became a norm. This tradition was later reaffirmed by the Council of Trent in 1563 and has been preserved up to the present. Thus, Catholics who enter the priesthood agree to a life of celibacy (Owen, 2001). This means that they cannot have families and raise children after ordination.

In Protestant churches, celibacy is not obligatory for their pastors and ministers. Protestant reformers argued that celibacy is contrary to biblical teaching (1Tim 4; 1-5; Heb 13:4 and 1Cor 9:5). Curiously, the RCC is the only Christian denomination which imposes mandatory clerical celibacy that is experiencing a worldwide condemnation today because of "scandalous" allegations of clerical sexual abuse (CSA) against women and children by priests and bishops. "Historically, scandals similar to these are known to have appeared only after mandatory celibacy laws were first instituted, centuries after Christ" (Daniel, 2012).

Although Protestant churches that allow married priesthood also experienced CSA among their ministers (e.g. Denney, Kerkey, and Gross, 2018), the extent and scope is not as intense and widespread compared to the Catholic Church's continuing clerical sexual misconduct worldwide. The United States (US) has an estimated 314,000 Protestant Christian congregations and a membership base of about 60 million (Grammich, 2012; Pew Research Center, 2007; Johnson et al., 2016). Although Protestant Christian congregations are both the most prevalent and frequently attended of all religious institutions within the US (Pew Research Center: Religion and Public Life 2015), research studies on instances of sexual abuse committed by their ministers have been sparse compared to the growing state investigations and research analyses against CSA by Catholic clerics. Thus, one wonders why Protestant and Christian Churches that allow married priesthood have lesser CSA cases compared to the RCC which imposes a universal obligatory celibacy to its clergy.

The widespread clerical sexual misconduct by Catholic priests was first made public after the Boston Globe's (2004) reports on the molestation of 130 boys by the Catholic priest John Geoghan from 1962 until 1993. Since then, more revelations of serious cases of clerical sexual abuse (CSA) have surfaced not just in the US but also in other parts of the world. Last February 2019, Pope Francis convened a sexual abuse summit attended by 200 top Church leaders from different continents and admitted that CSA is a global phenomenon in the RCC.

In response to the public outcry against CSA, the US bishops granted John Jay College in 2004 the unprecedented access to official RCC records in a commissioned study to understand the nature and extent of CSA in American dioceses, resulting in a finding that 4% of all priests within the US from 1950 to 2002 had some sexual abuse allegations made against them. It also showed that the alleged instances of sexual abuse involved nearly 11,000 children with only 3% of these cases were referred to law enforcement authorities (John Jay College, 2004).

The debate on the biblical and theological foundation of Catholic clerical celibacy has been going since the Second Lateran Council imposed it as a universal norm for priests in the 12th century. Assumptions relating celibacy with a lack of commitment to priestly life and ministry are not new to the RCC (Louden & Francis, 2003; Schoenherr & Vilarino, 1979). The mandatory celibacy of priests in the Latin rite even became one of the most provocative topics of the Second Vatican Council (Vatican II). In spite of the intense interest and debate on the biblical and doctrinal foundations of celibacy in the RCC, the fact remains that there are only a few empirical studies that relate celibacy and the priesthood, much more on the unintended consequences of the universal mandatory celibacy to CSA. Research studies on the negative effects of celibacy to priestly life rarely relate celibate life to the current clerical sexual misconduct.

Social Factors of CSA

The interest to do empirical studies on the causes of CSA in the RCC only received more attention lately after the international sexual abuse scandal began to unfold in 2002. Since 2002, much of the health-related scholarship about priests across disciplines such as psychology and psychiatry has focused on identifying and preventing CSA of minors (e.g., Plante 2003). It also focused on the psychological profile of predator priests as well as the negative effects of celibacy on the psychological health of priests. Plante and Aldridge (2005), for instance, found that clerical sexual offenders have profiles that tend to be defensive repressive, mistrustful, isolative, and irritable. While most of the research on sexual offenders has focused on the individual offenders and the etiology of their behavior, some recent works later begun to focus on the situations in which sexual abuse occurs and situational crime prevention techniques (Marshall, Serran, & Marshall, 2006; Wortley & Smallbone, 2006).

Pscyho-social research too on the well-being of priests began citing some situational and social factors that contribute to CSA. Rausch (1992), for instance, discovered that celibacy, loneliness, administrative pressures, and the lack of time management have adversarial effects on US priests (Rausch 1992). Virginia (1998) revealed that the US secular clergy is more depressed and emotionally exhausted in their ministry due to lack of social support networks and environments. This need for social support systems to boost self-esteem, positive moods, and higher perceived self-competence, and to foster a greater sense of belonging for people is supported by some studies (e.g., Meehan et al. 1993). Individuals with strong support networks are assumed to have a longer life expectancy, fewer stress-related disorders, and better-coping skills than otherwise (Antonovsky, 1979).

The search for a more sociological understanding of the social roots of CSA came with the empirical study of John Jay College of Criminal Justice (2004) on the causes and context of CSA. Although it did not blame mandatory celibacy as a major factor in clerical sexual misconduct, it did acknowledge that sexual deviance of priests is usually situational and opportunistic in nature rather than just negative psychological traits of individual priests. It noted that sexual abuse usually happens in unrestrained conditions wherein predator priests enjoy absolute privacy against their victims. This is consistent with the finding of Wortley & Smallbone (2006) which revealed that most sexual abuses occurred when the offender is alone with his victim, often in the home of the priest-offender or the victim where guardianship is absent.

The growing discovery of the rampant CSA in the US dioceses has resulted in the increase of academic studies attempting to uncover instances of sexual abuse within religious, primarily in Catholic, institutions. Prior to the Boston clerical scandal in 2002, only a few social scientists had attempted to do empirical studies on the prevalence of sexual abuse within the Catholic hierarchy (CH), particularly on the social and structural factors that facilitate CSA. The overwhelming majority of studies before 2002 on sexual abuse by priests primarily focused on either individual cases of abuse, how to stop abuse from occurring, how to recover from such instances of sexual abuse, or some combination of these issues (see Capps 1993, Flynn 2003, Horst 2000, Muse 1992, Poling 1999).

Sociological studies on the structural nature of CSA in the RCC are apparently absent. In particular, no sociological studies have seriously investigated the connection between mandatory clerical celibacy and the persistence of CSA in the diocesan clergy. Sociological analysis on the disorganizing effects of the universal obligatory celibacy to the social control of clerical behavior in the CH is also neglected. Yet, the widespread CSA in the US Catholic dioceses and in other parts of the world gave rise to a new wave of questions concerning the universal clerical celibacy in the RCC.

This chapter aims to argue that the universal mandatory clerical celibacy contributes to the social disorganization of the CH as a clerical community. It deprives the clergy of direct family social controls and informal supervisions necessary for an efficient and comprehensive social control of clerical behavior and inhibition of CSA, especially in the diocesan and parish levels of the CH.

Mandatory Celibacy and CSA

The current popular view on the causes of the persistence of CSA in the RCC emphasizes the moral and psychological weaknesses of the individual priests rather than the structural loopholes of the Church's social network and control systems as a result of the imposition of celibacy to priestly life. What surfaced in many lawsuits against predator priests is the admission of many bishops who think of CSA solely in terms of moral fault and sin (Doyle, 2006).

Despite the growing CSA around the world, the CH still refuses to view the universal mandatory clerical celibacy as a disorganizing factor in the diocesan priestly life which deprives the secular clergy of social support and direct social control of their behavior to resist CSA. Church authorities continue to understand CSA as mere moral and psychological aberrations of some problematic priests and bishops that need clinical treatment and spiritual direction.

Some prominent clerical writers do not also view the mandatory celibacy as connected to sexual misconduct by priests. Father Rosetti (2002), Father Martin (2017), and Greely (2004), for instance, argued that celibacy is not the cause of the current CSA, especially child clerical sexual abuse (cCSA). Responding to the views that priests are more likely to be child molesters than others because they are celibate and that a celibate priesthood attracts a larger proportion of men with sexual problems, the priest-research professor and consultant to the papal Commission on the Protection of Minors Father Stephen Rosetti did not see mandatory celibacy as the cause of CSA and cCSA. He argued that researchers and clinicians have generally accepted the fact that celibacy does not cause child sexual abuse because the sexual difficulties and inner psychological problems that give rise to cCSA are largely in place long before a person enters into the formation process for a celibate priesthood.

Father Martin too argued that celibacy is not the cause of CSA since celibacy does not cause pedophilia. To him, blaming celibacy is an enormous simplification that leaves out many important causes. He then enumerated some major causes of the CSA: First, improper screening of candidates for seminaries led to some psychologically sick men being ordained as priests. When some bishops received reports of sexual abuse, the reports were tragically downplayed, dismissed or ignored. Second, the crimes of sexual abuse often went unreported to civil authorities, out of a misguided concern among church officials for "avoiding scandal," the fear of litigation, or an unwillingness to confront the abusive priest. Third, grossly misunderstanding the severity of the effects of abuse, overly relying on advice from psychologists regarding rehabilitation, and privileging the concerns of priests over the pastoral care for victims, some bishops moved abusive priests from one parish to another where they repeatedly offended (Martin, 2017).

Finally, the sociologist-priest Father Andrew Greely (2004) also dismissed the view that celibacy is to be blamed for the current CSA and cCSA in the RCC. This is his reaction to the argument to what he considered a simplistic view: 4% of Catholic priests are abusers; priests are committed to celibacy; therefore, frustrations of celibate life led to abuse and celibacy must be abolished. Greely argued that most experts in sexual abuse of minors and children attribute CSA to a deep and incurable syndrome acquired early in life. Married priesthood won't cure it. An abuser who marries is a married abuser (Greely, 2003).

These three clerical authors have rightly argued that clerical celibacy is not the direct cause of CSA in the RCC. Thus, abolishing celibacy for priests won't stop the current clerical sexual misconduct. The obligatory celibacy is not the immediate cause of the CSA. They are also right to say that celibacy does not produce pedophilia. These authors, however, authors were just responding to the view that simplifies a complex issue. Thus, this chapter argues that clerical celibacy is not the proximate and immediate cause of CSA but its main contributory structural factor for the persistence of CSA in the RCC, whether it involves minors, adolescents, or adults, both male and female. Celibacy provides diocesan clerics absolute privacy and deprives them of direct social control which can be performed by family members if a married priesthood, whether heterosexual or same-sex marriage, is allowed in the RCC. Married priesthood can greatly regulate priestly behavior and minimize opportunities for CSA. Pedophilia and cCSA could not be resolved by married priesthood, but by strict screening of candidates to the priesthood in the seminary and immediate dismissal from the clerical state for those guilty of cCSA.

The causes mentioned above by Fr. Martin only underscore the lack of lay participation in the internal affairs of the RCC. The screening of candidates, downplaying, dismissal, or ignoring of clerical sexual crimes are not done by the laity but by bishops who have the authority to discipline erring priests in the diocese. Furthermore, the avoidance of scandal by covering up CSA cases as well as reliance on psychologists and psychiatrists are common patterns done by bishops and not by the laity who has no power to deal with abusive priests.

Celibacy is not the proximate cause of CSA but its ultimate cause. From the point of view of law enforcement or behavioral control theories, celibacy hinders the wider regulation of clerical behavior by the laity which can minimize opportunities for sexual deviance. It ultimately prevents effective clerical behavior as it disables the laity to participate in the internal management of the Church and monitor clerical behavior to prevent sexual misconduct.

The RCC requires ordination, which is inseparable to celibacy, to participate in ecclesiastical governance. This celibacy requirement obstructs the genuine lay empowerment in the RCC which can greatly minimize CSA. Celibacy is the main stumbling block to the laity's capability to fight CSA, as Vatican II recognized the lay Catholics as experts in the secular world such as the surveillance of clerical behavior and identifying CSA. It also facilitates absolute privacy for clerical life and allows clerical deviance without the active regulation of priestly behavior by the laity which constitutes 99.9% of the total Catholic population.

CSA is usually done in absolute privacy with priests who are usually alone with their victims. Compared to religious priesthood, diocesan priesthood lacks an intimate clerical community which can provide mutual support and direct monitoring of clerical behavior. Child sexual abuse by pedophile priests is only a small percentage of the total cases of CSA in which the most common type is sexual abuse by heterosexual or homosexual priests against adolescents and adults, such as rapes of nuns by priests, a type of CSA which is not the focus of the current investigations and media reports. Thus, a universal married priesthood can be an appropriate response to this type of sexual abuse as family life can provide direct supervision or behavioral control of clerical behavior.

Published reports of some credible investigative bodies singled out the obligatory celibacy in the RCC as one of the major causes of the endurance of CSA. A comprehensive study that looked at the findings of 26 royal commissions and other inquiries from Australia, Ireland, the UK, Canada, and the Netherlands since 1985, for instance, mentioned mandatory celibacy as one major factor that caused high rates of CSA in the RCC. In particular, Australia's royal commission's final report saw a connection between CSA and mandatory celibacy and recommended to the Australian Bishops Conference to consider introducing voluntary celibacy to diocesan clergy. It argued that mandatory celibacy contributed to CSA when combined with other risk factors. It also mentioned that compulsory celibacy has contributed to various forms of psychological dysfunctions, including psychosexual immaturity, which poses an ongoing risk to the safety of children.[1]

The John Jay College, which was commissioned by American bishops to study the persistence of CSA in 2004, saw connections in the literature between CSA and social isolation and loneliness, subjective states, and vulnerabilities of priests which can be alleviated if celibacy is optional (John Jay College, 2004). In his book "A Secret World: Sexuality and the Search for Celibacy" which documented case files and 25 years of interviews with hundreds of sexually active priests and victims of CSA, Richard Sipe also singled out obligatory celibacy as a major contributory factor in the persistence of CSA in the RCC. He estimated that probably more than half of all celibate priests were sexually active and that six percent of them had been involved with minors (Sipe, 1990). He warned the Church officials that when men in authority—cardinals, bishops, rectors, abbots, confessors, professors—are having or have had an unacknowledged active sex life under the guise of celibacy, an atmosphere of tolerance of CSA within the system is made operative.

This warning pointed out the structural roots of CSA which can have adverse effects to clerical behavior. Unfortunately, Sipe's warning fell on deaf ears and widely criticized by church officials who insisted that celibacy was not the problem in the persistence of CSA (The Baltimore Sun, 24 Aug 2018).[2] Bishops primarily view clerical sexual misconduct as a psychological problem of some priests and not a structural problem which has a connection to the mandatory clerical celibacy.

Thus, one may inquire: Is the universal mandatory clerical celibacy for Catholic priests a major social disorganizing factor in the persistence of CSA in the RCC? Does it contribute to the social disorganization of the CH as a community and weaken the social control of clerical behavior resulting in the prevalence of CSA?

---

[1]Royal Commission into Institutional Responses to Sexual Abuse of Children, "Final Report Recommedations. Retrieved Dec. 1, 2018 from https://www.childabuseroyalcommission.gov.au/sites/default/files/final_report_recommendations.pdf.

[2]http://www.baltimoresun.com/news/maryland/dan-rodricks-blog/bs-md-rodricks-0826-story.html.

Social Disorganization Theory and Clerical Sexual Abuse

Most theories which study the persistence of crime in communities assess the level of social bonding of members as well as the existence of direct and indirect social controls which regulate individual behavior. One of the known sociological theories on crime that aims to explain the endurance of deviance in communities is the social disorganization theory (SDT). Social disorganization has been defined by sociologists as the "the inability of a community structure to realize the common values of its residents and maintain effective social controls" (Kornhauser, 1978:63). The SDT became popular in the 1940s with the work of the early Chicago-research school scholars (e.g., Shaw & McKay 1942).

The classical SDT explanation on the dominance of crime in communities pointed to the ecological conditions as primarily shaping crimes rates over and above the characteristics of individual residents.[3] This was, however, reformulated in subsequent years starting with the seminal works of Kornhauser (1978), Stark (1987), Bursik (1988), Sampson & Groves (1989), and Bursik & Grasmick (1993) which focused on the informal social control and the collective ability of neighborhoods to intervene and supervise residents to maintain public order (Sampson et al., 1997, 1999). It assumed that the weakening of informal control mechanisms can disable neighborhoods to control crime.[4]

In general, the SDT emphasizes the importance of direct and indirect social controls in communities and neighborhoods to prevent crime and deviance. It provides three sources of disorganization, namely: residential mobility that disrupts a community network of relations (Kornhauser, 1978), racial and ethnic heterogeneity that weakens the mediating components of social organization, especially control of disorderly behavior, and marital and family disruption which can decrease indirect social controls at the community levels.

The current social disorganization research is built on the notion that well-developed local network structures reduce crime. This formulation is grounded in the systemic model of community organization, which views the local community "as a complex system of friendship and kinship networks and formal and informal associational ties rooted in family life and ongoing socialization processes" (Kasarda & Morris, 1974, p. 329; Bursik, 1988; Bursik & Grasmick, 1993; Sampson & Groves, 1989). Obligatory clerical celibacy, especially for diocesan clergy who, unlike the religious clergy, live independently in parishes and dioceses with no religious communities to support them, has effectively created a socially disorganized clerical community with weak direct control for priestly behavior.

---

[3] Charis E. Kubrin and Ronald Wiezer, "New Directions in Social Disorganization Theory" *Journal of Research of Crime and Deliquency.* (November 2003), 374–75.

[4] Fred E. Marcowitz, et al., "Extending Social Disorganization Theory: Modeling the Cohesion between Relationships, Disorder, and Fear". Criminology 2, 9, (May 2009), 293–94.

Marital and family disruptions are seen to decrease informal social controls at the community level. Severe disorganization can even occur in communities of celibate men with active sexuality and without family life. One basic thesis of SDT is that two-parent households provide increased supervision and guardianship not only between the spouses but also to the children (Cohen & Felson, 1979), as well as the general activities of the community. From this perspective, the supervision of crime and rule-breaking behavior is not only dependent on rule-breaker's family, but also on a collective network of family control in the community (Thrasher, 1963; Reis, 1986).

Though criticized for not being directly tested due to lack of direct and relevant data to provide measures for the variables hypothesized (Sampson & Groves, 1989), the SDT is, nevertheless, seen by some researchers as useful in ethnographic studies as it provides rich descriptive accounts of community processes central to theoretical concerns, albeit limited in theory testing. Most qualitative studies using the SDT, however, focus on a single community or, at most a cluster of neighborhoods that do not display variation (Reis, 1986; Sampson & Groves, 1989). Due to its structural approach in analyzing crimes in communities, scholars started to use the SDT to assess the social roots of sexual abuse by priests and religious leaders in religious communities and churches (e.g., Rose 2000, Denney 2015).

One important thesis of the reformulated SDT is that direct and indirect social controls are necessary to inhibit deviance and crime in a community or organization. The current literature on the Catholic priesthood has not adequately employed the sociological perspective and explore the negative unintended consequences of mandated celibacy on the communal life and social control of clerical behavior. It has not examined the social disorganizing effect of mandated celibacy to the social control of priestly behavior. It has not adequately assessed the consequences of the universal celibacy to clericalism, and loose monitoring of priestly behavior against CSA.

Canon 277 of the CCL on the mandatory celibacy for Catholic priests imposes a seemingly impossible task, namely, living a perfect and perpetual continence for Catholic priests. Although the church propagates the belief that bishops and priests are celibate, this is totally not based on fact. Several modern studies have used various methods to measure the degree of celibate observance.[5] But no researcher so far has assessed that more than 50% of Roman Catholic clergy at any one time are, in fact, practicing celibacy (Sipe, 2010).

---

[5]For example, based on the personal experience of the author as a seminarian for more than 7 years and interviews with key informants of the study, it is estimated that out of more than a hundred priests in one diocese of Mindanao in the Philippines, only around 10 or less are perceived to be observing celibacy.

Mandatory Celibacy and the Social Status of Clerics

Diocesan priests promise to live a celibate and chaste life that is prohibitive of marriage and sexual behavior in order to facilitate priests' full devotion of service to the Church (Issaco, Sahker, & Krinock, 2015). Celibacy implies complete sexual abstinence and renouncement of marriage in clerical life.

One major argument in favor of celibacy is the view that mandated celibacy can make priests more spiritual compared to married clergy. It has also been argued, using several biblical texts and traditional statements, that celibacy is a better choice and enables a priest to be more devoted to God as it frees him from concerns of marriage and children and makes him more mature in spirituality. But an earlier study by Swenson (1998) involving a database of 1294 evangelical ministers (most of whom are married) and 80 Catholic priests in Canada revealed that being celibate did not make a significant difference to one's spiritual life.

There is also a shred of ample historical evidence to clearly demonstrate that priests, bishops, cardinals, and popes remain human in spite of the vow of celibacy and the sacred ceremonies that elevate them to their lofty positions. Priests and bishops, in spite of ordination, are no different than mere mortals (Doyle, 2006). Ordination only makes clerics a privileged group in the RCC, providing them with sacramental and political powers in the church administration. They are in no way superior to the laity as spiritual beings in the RCC just because of ordination and celibacy.

The resistance against optional celibacy and married priesthood can be seen as connected with the lofty social stature of priests in the CH. Clerics will gradually step down from their pedestals once the RCC allows marriage to those who want to enter the clerical state. Clerics would no longer be that distinct in the RCC compared to the laity who is usually married with a family. Abandoning the universal clerical celibacy or allowing optional celibacy can diminish the clergy's power and prestige, as well as clericalism, in the RCC. Moreover, removing the obligatory celibacy would make Catholic priests not significantly different from their Protestant and Christian counterparts who are usually married in their churches.

In the wake of the challenges raised in the context of the acceptance of married pastors of non-Roman Catholic communities into the Catholic priesthood, Francis T. Hurley, the Archbishop of Anchorage, Alaska, for instance, asserted that the mandate of celibacy in the Latin Church is attractive because it is an element in the identity of the priest in the RCC, as well as a sign of the charism of the diocesan priest (America 28 Feb 1998). In this case, celibacy confers a special or "celebrity" status for clerics, elevating their social stature in the RCC, higher than that of the married laity. Thus, abandoning the universal obligatory celibacy and allowing married priesthood would diminish the Catholic priest's social status in the RCC and undermine clericalism or the "cult of the priest" in the Christian community—something that is probably too costly for some top clerics who get used to power and privilege in the hierarchical Church.

There are no comprehensive and scientific studies on the total number of ordained priests and bishops who practice celibacy. But it is common knowledge among priests and seminarians that only a few priests and bishops practice celibacy while in the active ministry (Sipe, 2010). Daniel (2012) estimated that only ten percent of all priests and bishops successfully abstain from sex during their priesthood. Ninety percent of clerics engage in sex: 50% continuously and 40% periodically. Of those, 30–50% are homosexuals and their sexual activity is comparable to heterosexual priests and bishops. Similar studies from Spain, Switzerland, South Africa, and the Philippines, produced similar numbers. In areas of South America and Africa, more than half of all priests are said to have wives/mistresses. Double lives on all levels of clerical life are tolerated if they do not cause scandal or raise legal problems in the RCC. Sexual activity between bishops and priests and adult partners is well known within clerical circles (Sipe, 2010).

Although many clerics disregard celibacy in social practice, being unmarried nevertheless provides them with higher social status and power over the laity as they appear being role models of Christian life that resembles that of Christ who was celibate during his life. By abandoning marriage and family life for priests, the RCC has created the CH as a unique form of human community whose members are unmarried or celibate. By maintaining the universal celibacy, the RCC inadvertently protects clericalism and adopts a socially-disorganized, all-male celibate community without intermediary and direct social controls which can be provided by families, wives, and/or children in a universal optional celibacy.

Celibacy and Clericalism

The RCC is the only Christian Church which imposes the mandatory celibacy to its clergy with a high level of clericalism in its ecclesiastical culture. Pope Francis has repeatedly warned priests on the negative effects of clericalism. He blamed the current CSA scandal to clericalism but not to celibacy. To him, clericalism, whether fostered by priests themselves or by laypersons, can lead to an excision in the ecclesial body that supports and helps to perpetuate many of the evils in the church: A 'no' to abuse to him is to say 'no' to all forms of clericalism (Biblefalseprofit.com, 2018).

Clericalism is understood by Doyle (2006) as "the radical misunderstanding of the place of clerics (deacons, priests, bishops) in the Catholic Church and in secular society... [an] erroneous belief that clerics constitute an elite group and, because of their powers as sacramental ministers, they are superior to the laity" (p. 190). "The common conception, evident from theological and catechetical writings, church law, and liturgical practice, is that bishops are direct descendants of the apostles and both bishops and priests are ontologically different from lay persons because they have been singled out by God to represent Jesus Christ on earth" (Doyle, 2006, p.194). What separates clerics from the laity aside from ordination is the universal mandatory celibacy since only celibate priests can celebrate the Sacrament of the Eucharist, seen by Catholics as the summit of Christian life and the center of Catholic spirituality.

The RCC imposes the mandatory celibacy to all priests and bishops, making them leaders and uniquely different from the laity in the Christian community. Celibacy creates clericalism by making priests and bishops metaphysically different from the married and non-ordained laity. Although celibacy is a church-created law (universally imposed at the Second Lateran Council in 1139) and not grounded in scripture, it has traditionally been framed by Church authorities in such a way that it appears to be essential to the authentic priesthood and clerical life (John Paul II, 2002). It provides a sense of fullness of spiritual attainment that is seen as largely reserved to ordained ministers of the RCC.

> While celibacy for clergy remains a disciplinary not doctrinal matter, its theological justification is popular in the universal church, including the idea that the priest follows the model of Jesus Christ, whose spouse is the Church. With this conception, the RCC views clerics as the only real, full examples of religious life, while lay people mostly occupy a second-best, helper status (Blakely, 2018).

Thus, Doyle (2006) sees celibacy as a "kind of clerical garb that fortifies the illusion that clerics are ontologically superior, setting them apart from the laity, enhancing the wall of secrecy, and adding to the mystique about the clerical world" (p. 196).

The universal clerical celibacy cannot also be seen as the reason for the shortage of priests in the RCC. Campion (2001) argued that the demand for celibacy is not the major reason for the shortage of priests because it is an experience of Roman Catholicism that retains priestly celibacy. Clericalism which sees ordained clerics as a "special" group or political elite in the hierarchical Church can be a major reason why mandated celibacy is retained in the RCC. Celibacy creates a mindset among the laity that the ordained priests are "special role models of Christian life in the Church as they imitate Christ's celibacy and ministry. Traditional Catholic culture associated celibacy with the heroic asceticism of the clergy whose ecclesial and social status was largely unquestioned" (Sheldrake, 1994, p. 29).

Despite the fact that they constitute only a minuscule fraction (0.00042%) of the world's Catholic population, celibate and male clerics, especially bishops, exercise monarchial powers in the RCC liable only to the Pope. They constitute the "ruling class" in the institutional church. No married clerics, lay people, or women hold any positions of power or influence anywhere in the RCC (Doyle, 2006). And since there is no separation of powers between executive, legislative, and judicial branches within the Church, celibate clerics exercise absolute powers in ecclesiastical governance. Thus, the CH constitutes of what political scientists call "the leadership elite" of the RCC, a unique sub-group that rules the RCC with a membership of more than one billion around the world. In the minds of many, the Church is even synonymous with the clergy (Doyle, 2006). This mindset benefits altogether the abusive heterosexual, homosexual, and pedophile priests who view themselves as a privileged celibate class in the Church which can embolden them to persist in their CSA without a strong social control from the religious and laity.

The Christ-like life and spirituality provided by a celibate priesthood could not be an important justification for maintaining the obligatory celibacy for priests. Despite the dominant clericalist ideology that conditions the mind of many Catholics in the RCC, empirical studies do not see a significant difference in spirituality and commitment between celibate and married priesthood. Sheldrake (1994), for instance argued, that the mandatory clerical celibacy is only a reflection of the superstructure of celibate culture that sees human intimacy as a distraction of one's attention from God. In today's mature consciousness, sexuality-interpreted-as-lust has been replaced by sexuality-as-relatedness. Thus, those who suggest that issues of celibacy are mere 'hormone problems' ignore the fact that the positive values of relatedness and collaboration are increasingly described as at the heart of sexuality. Clerical celibacy is, therefore, alienating clerics from the positive values of intimacy, relatedness, mutual support as crucial in developing healthy human sexuality which can inhibit CSA in the RCC (Sheldrake 1994).

The Catholic Hierarchy and Bridging Social Networks

The Catholic clergy lacks formal and informal social controls within the CH social networks as well as those that connect the different diocesan and parochial communities or what Putnam (2000) calls as "bridging social capital" or network of connections that crosscut different members of different groups.[6] This lack of bridging networks in the CH can weaken the institutional social control which can result in the prevalence of CSA. There are few lay organizations which directly help priests in distress as well as clerical support groups which can immediately help lonely priests in the parishes.

Hoge's (2002) study confirmed the perception that newly ordained priests find priestly life difficult and discouraging. He identified the four most common reasons for leaving the priesthood: falling in love, rejecting celibacy, experiencing disillusion, and feeling rejected as a gay person. He argued that loneliness has a direct effect on the resignation of priests from the active ministry and mediates other factors involved in the decision to remain in and to leave the priesthood (Sunardi, 2014). According to the National Association of Church Personnel Administrators, which surveyed dioceses and religious orders as part of a project, about 10–15% of priests resigned in the first five years after ordination due to loneliness (pp. 16–17). Clancy (2008) captures the loneliness and difficult situations faced by newly-ordained priests:

> [T]he newly ordained priest is expected by many to be the "expert" and due to his role in the community, it is difficult for him to know where to turn for support or who to confide in regarding his difficulties. While the pastor might seem to be the most obvious person for him to confide in, it is unusual for him to turn to him. The pastor is his "boss", they live together, they work in close proximity, often there is a degree of competition between them, and there is often a very large difference in age, philosophy/theology, and experience. At the time that the newly ordained priest most needs a place to turn to mine the rich experiences that he is having he finds himself alone (p. 35).

Thus, to address the loneliness in the parish, newly-ordained priests, especially in the US, started to affiliate with clerical support groups to fill their need for

---

[6]Robert D. Putnam, *Bowling Alone: The Collapse and Revival of American Community*, New York: Simon and Schuster (2000).

companionship and mutual support. Thus, one of the major recommendations of Hoge's study (2002) is for the RCC to encourage support programs and gatherings of priests where they can share their experiences, "support groups that discuss real issues, not just exchange pleasantries (p. 50)." Diocesan priesthood does not provide direct guardianship and mutual support from the clerical community against 'temptations' and serious personal crises experienced by priests in the ministry. The Church teachings strongly emphasize unity and collegiality of the clergy as sharing one priesthood of Christ. But the current ecclesiastical set-up and the CCL provide an atomistic structure of the CH where the dioceses under the local bishops acquire vast ecclesiastical powers, autonomous from each other, without being supervised by the laity, and subject only to the Roman Pontiff's control.

Church documents always teach that the CH is a community, a collegial body, sharing the same priesthood of Christ and united as one community of pastors under the leadership of the pope in the RCC. Despite the emphasis of church documents on communal unity of the clergy, there is apparent lack of formal and informal intermediary organizations that regularly connect the various diocesan and parochial communities of bishops, priests, and deacons with the Roman Curia and the pope in Rome, especially on matters indirectly related to pastoral or administrative work such as personal, psychological, and cultural concerns.

The CH's lack of intermediary networks which provide informal social control in the diocesan and parish life for the secular clergy is hindered by the mandatory clerical celibacy. The current set-up of the CH reveals that clerics are relatively living autonomous lives in their own dioceses and parishes. There is a lack formal and informal support groups that mediate the parish life of the priests and diocesan bishops, just as the bishops with the Roman Curia and the pope. One informant of one study by Clancy (2008) provides an insight of the need for diocesan priests to live with an intimate group either through marriage and family life or a religious community to lead a healthy and normal priestly life:

> One monk was studying with us…he was criticizing celibacy. His point was a good one. He said in the Orthodox Church a man does not live alone. You are either married and have a family or you are a monk and live in a community. There is no concept of living alone. Being alone doesn't work. Being married isn't the only answer, but you know, being a healthy celibate is being supported by other celibates who understand your vocation, and living with them is healthy. People will object, but guys should be formed to live in communities. We have to form men to live in a community. Now, not that we will be religious, we will still be diocesan priests (p. 122).

With the lack of opportunities for social interaction, social bonding, and proactive monitoring for the laity against CSA, bishops and priests live a relatively unrestrained life, without intimate groups such as families which can strengthen clerical social bonds and inhibit deviance. As already mentioned in previous chapters, the presbyterium in the diocese and the episcopal conference cannot serve as intimate groups for priests and bishops to provide direct and indirect clerical social control against CSA. The clerical communal activities are insufficient for secular priests and bishops to experience a strong social bonding and mutual support to fight against CSA. Thus, one wonders whether marriage and family life which are suppressed by the universal clerical obligatory celibacy is one of the missing bridging social capitals that can strengthen the social bonds of the clergy and increase social control against CSA.

Research studies on CSA have shown that several sexual misconduct by diocesan clergy were done in situations where priests are unrestrained in their personal behavior, without effective guardians who can supervise their daily behavior. The bishop is usually a distant figure and co-pastors often do not interfere in the personal behavior of their fellow priests. One priest in one diocese in the Philippines, for instance, who is known to take illegal drugs, asked to be assigned to a particular parish as a resident priest because the parish priest is his personal friend and who is tolerant of his misbehavior in the diocese.[7]

One priest also revealed in one interview that priests are usually secretive and protective of the misconduct to their fellow priests. They usually take the attitude of non-interference concerning the deviant conduct of their fellow priests, unless the bishop requires their cooperation in an investigation. This implies that priests cannot effectively act as guardians against the CSA of their brother priests. In the absence of formal powers of the laity to investigate and sanction clerical misbehavior and with the universal mandatory celibacy, there is no clear guardians who can supervise the daily behavior of priests and prevent clerical deviance.

CSA is often done secretly and unreported to bishops. Informants agreed that priests who committed abuses usually do not report their crimes to their bishops. It is easy for them to hide their crime in a confession with their fellow priests and ask for forgiveness without the fear of being exposed publicly due to the seal of confession. Under the CCL, a priest who reveals the sin and the sinner in a confession is automatically excommunicated by the RCC. Unless the abuse is reported by the victim or his/her relatives directly to the bishop, or has become a public scandal, the bishop would not know about the CSA case. The seal of confession inadvertently contributes to the secrecy of CSA cases in the RCC.

The lack of intermediary groups between the bishop and priests which monitor the daily whereabouts of clerics provides more deviant opportunities for predator priests. Thus, the family, if married priesthood or optional universal clerical celibacy is allowed, can provide a direct social control to the daily behavior of priests which can prevent clerical misconduct. The spouses and children of the married priests can extend mutual support and informal monitoring of clerical behavior against CSA in their ministries. Familial ties among priests and bishops can also lead to a greater informal social control against CSA.

The two most common scenarios in CSA are: (1) the abuse occurs in a private setting and (2) the private setting chosen is typically the offender's home (Wortley & Smallbone, 2006). Only a few studies have identified the typical place clerical sexual misconduct usually occurs. But John Jay College report (2004) showed that 41% of all the alleged sexual abuse happened within the priest's home. With celibacy and the

---

[7]Based on the author's personal interview of a key informant who is personally close to these two priests and their former con-seminarian during their formation years.

lack of clerical supervision by the CH, the predator priest has more opportunities to be alone with their victims in the rectory or convent. Thus, if marriage and family life are allowed for diocesan priests, total privacy would be eliminated and sexual abuse in the priest's home can be prevented. Moreover, the priest's wife and children could also provide increased guardianship in the parish and serve as deterrence against CSA.

Marriage and Social Control of Clerical Abuse

One universal trait that has been found in earlier studies concerning sexual misconduct and abuse is that the overwhelming majority of known offenders are male (Francis & Baldo, 1998; Friberg & Laaser, 1998; Garland & Argueta, 2010; Thoburn & Whitman, 2004). This characteristic should not come as a surprise since most Christian denominations (88%) only allow males to assume leadership positions within the church (Cooperative Congregations Studies Partnership, 2010).

One important fact found in most CSA cases is that only a small percentage of abusers are believed to have some form of paraphilia, which is an extreme fixation on a certain individual, object, or situation that results in intense sexual arousal (American Psychiatric Association, 2013). In the RCC, many cases of CSA are committed by either gay or heterosexual celibate priests. Pedophile priests who commit child abuse present a different case that cannot be addressed by married or optional celibate priesthooda but by an outright dismissal from the priesthood. There are many forms of sexual abuse by homosexual priests against males and heterosexual priests against adolescent and female adults which are not being included in the current focus of CSA investigations by authorities and the media.

Child sexual abuse (cCSA) by gay priests constitutes only a small percentage of all clerical sexual abuses by diocesan clergy. "Although the present chapter in the age-old drama of problematic celibacy has often been referred to as a 'pedophile crisis' the evidence thus far shows that true pedophiles constitute about 20% of the offenders, while the remaining sexual abuse victims have been adolescents or vulnerable adults" (Doyle, 2006). Married priesthood, whether heterosexual or homosexual, can then greatly provide increased guardianship against CSA committed by the majority of celibate and heterosexual priests. Gay priests in the CH can even be helped against CSA if the RCC allows gay clerical marriages as some gay priests and bishops maintain illicit union and affairs with men. The cCSA of pedophile priests, however, presents a different case since it involves some psychological and psychiatric problems which cannot be addressed by a universal married priesthood but by a strict screening of candidates to the priesthood and outright dismissal from the clerical state as stipulated in the CCL.

The prerequisite for a family to function as a source of social control in any society is that it should be intact and functional as an institution. The family should be a source of affection for its members and it should give them an identity and a sense of social acceptance. Marriage and family life provide the necessary direct and formal social controls which can prevent crime and deviance. Social control can be understood as a system of 'measures, suggestion, persuasion, restraint and coercion' by which society brings people into conformity with an accepted code of behavior (Sharma, 2007, p. 220). Social control comes in two distinct forms. It can be direct or indirect.

Direct social control works when someone exerts influence on a person directly due to their close proximity such as members of one's immediate family. Spouses and children can monitor the whereabouts of any member of the family. Umberson (1987) argues that the indirect influence of social control as experienced through informal pressures to conform is exerted primarily through the family. Thus, the married priesthood can provide the priest direct control to conform to ecclesiastical norms through the guardianship of his spouse and/or children. It can also limit absolute privacy and thus minimize the opportunities for CSA.

Celibacy can deprive diocesan priests of familial direct social control and leave them lonely with complete privacy. There are anecdotal evidences that showed that some diocesan priests would slip out from the parish anonymous and undetected with their tinted luxury cars to visit prostitution houses, nightclubs, gay bars, and other prohibited places. In the Philippines, one senior diocesan priest was arrested by local police for attempting to bring a minor in his heavily-tinted sports utility vehicle to a nearby motel. There are even priests in the country who regularly visit cockpits and gamble.

The CCL has explicitly enjoined clerics to refrain completely from all things which are unbecoming to their state (Canon 285, 1) and to avoid those things which, although not unbecoming, are nevertheless foreign to the clerical state (Canon 285, 2). It also requires them to live a life of simplicity and refrain from all things that have a semblance of vanity (Canon 282, 1). Vices, vanities, and sexual escapades by priests could be hindered by spouses and children if a universal married priesthood is allowed in the RCC. A family is a primary group and, as an institution, it provides direct behavioral supervision of the members which can discourage deviance. In the absence of family life as a result of obligatory celibacy, the diocesan priest only avails of the weak indirect social controls from a dispersed hierarchical community of clerics.

Indirect social control is said to be provided by factors removed physically from the person, such as institutions, traditions, customs, and culture. Indirect means of social control are 'invisible and subtle' (Sharma, 2007, p. 221). The CH offers only limited indirect social controls to clerics. The presbyterium or council of priests as a secondary group can only provide minimal indirect control as its members seldom see each other due to limited communal activities and pastoral workload. Religious associations that offer spiritual and mutual support to clerics are also scarce. Despite the canonical provision that bishops must take full control of their clergy's discipline, local ordinaries remain relatively distant from their diocesan priests. Bishops can only extend minimal direct and indirect social control to clerical behavior as they are usually preoccupied with personal, pastoral administrative concerns in their dioceses.

In a universal married priesthood, the networks of families, relatives, and friends of the priests and bishops can also provide a strong indirect social control which increases the regulation of clerical behavior and social cohesiveness of the CH.

The family has always been seen in the social sciences as a strong means of social control that monitors the behavior of its members in society against deviance. Juvenile delinquency, for instance, is often attributed to a lack of family and parental supervision to children. Early studies using social disorganization theories (e.g., Gove & Crutchfield 1982, Van Voorhis et al. 1988) and the social bond model of Hirschi (1969) have shown that the family is an effective means of social control against criminal behavior. Recent studies also revealed the crucial role of the family social bond in preventing various forms of misconduct. These researches recognized supportive parenting behaviors as negatively linked to delinquency, indicating that high levels of support and warmth of parents are associated with low levels of delinquency, while low levels or even rejection are connected to high levels of deviance (e.g., Barnes & Farrell 1992, Juang & Silbereisen 1999, Simons, Robertson, & Downs, 1989).

Marital and family relations and networks as a result of a married priesthood can provide what Putnam (2000) labeled as bridging and bonding social capitals. The former is linked to what social network theorists and researchers refer to as "weak ties," which are loose connections between individuals who may provide useful information or new perspectives for one another, but typically not emotional support (Granovetter, 1982). Bonding social capital is found between individuals in tightly knit, emotionally close relationships, such as family and close friends. Married priesthood can make the CH more cohesive as families and friends of married clerics can serve as a bridging social capital between parishes and dioceses and at the same time, as a bonding social capital which provides priests intimacy and emotional support to resist CSA.

Extensive research on the prevalence of crime in a community is associated with the absence and breakdown of family relations that can lead to various forms of crime. Mandatory celibacy which removes family relations and their consequent direct social controls in clerical life can be a major social disorganizing factor in the CH as a community of religious leaders. It can result in a weak social control system of priestly behavior in the CH against CSA. Obligatory universal celibacy in the CH is also an important reason why the diocesan clergy often live autonomous and anonymous personal lives. There are no lay intermediaries such as family associations and kinship networks of clerics that can connect one parish or diocese to another and provide social controls against deviance. With the absence of lay councils or boards with real ecclesiastical and political powers to monitor clerical behavior and sanction CSA, clerics are predominantly unrestrained in their personal behavior and clerical life in the dioceses and parishes.

Lastly, a married priesthood can lead to more social networks in the CH which strengthen social ties and result in a greater supervision of clerical behavior. Resources such as obligations, information, trust, and norms transmitted through social ties among families of a community are key to facilitating social control (Kubrin & Weitzer, 2003). Ties between neighboring spouses or parents, for example, may lead to the sharing of information or mutual obligations (resources) that may serve as a basis for monitoring and controlling behavior. In this case, the family networks of a universal married priesthood can intensify the social cohesiveness of the CH and prevent CSA in the RCC.

Summary

This chapter has illustrated the connection between the universal mandatory clerical celibacy in the RCC and the social disorganization of the CH as a community. Despite the lack of biblical and doctrinal basis and research studies on the negative effects of celibacy to clerical life, celibacy remained a norm in the RCC for clerics. The universal obligatory clerical celibacy can be a social disorganizing factor in the RCC as it deprives the diocesan clergy direct and indirect controls to clerical behavior. Child sexual abuse committed by the clergy only constitutes a small percentage of CSA. The majority are committed by celibate heterosexual or homosexual diocesan clerics—empirically shown by some studies–who are generally lonely in their parishes and living in absolute privacy, secrecy in sexual matters, and autonomy in their personal life. A universal married priesthood with optional celibacy can provide clerics with direct social control of behavior as spouses and children can extend a strong guardianship against CSA. The various marital and family networks in the parishes and dioceses as a consequence of married priesthood can increase social ties and intermediary networks in the CH, leading to a greater social control and deterrence against CSA.

References

Abbott, E. A. (2001). *A history of celibacy*. Cambridge, UK: Lutterworth Press.

American Psychiatric Association (2013). *Diagnostic and statistical manual of mental disorders, fifth edition*. Washington, DC: American Psychiatric Association Publishing.

Antonovsky, A. (1979). *Health, stress, and coping*. San Francisco: Josey-Bass.

Barnes, G. M., & Farrell, M. P. (1992). Parental support and control as predictors of adolescent drinking, delinquency, and related problem behaviors. *Journal of Marriage and the Family, 54*(4), 763–776.

Biblefalseprophet.com. (2018). Francis on sex abuse: It's "clericalism" and you laity should do penance. Retrieved December 13, 2018 from https://biblefalseprophet.com/2018/08/21/francis-on-sex-abuse-its-clericalism-and-you-laity-should-do-penance/.

Blakely, J. (2018, December 13). Sexual abuse and the culture of clericalism. *America*. https://www.americamagazine.org/faith/2018/08/23/sexual-abuse-and-culture-clericalism.

Bursik, R. J., Jr. (1988). Social disorganization and theories of crime and delinquency: Problems and prospects. *Criminology, 26*, 519–551.

Bursik, R. J., Jr., & Grasmick, H. G. (1993). *Neighborhoods and crime*. New York: Lexington Books.

Campion, O. F. (2001). Vocations and culture. *The Priest, 57*(7), 384.

Capps, D. (1993). Sex in the parish: Social-scientific explanations for why it occurs. *The Journal of Pastoral Care, 47*(4), 350–361.

Clancy, R. (2008). *The perceptions of the recently ordained priests of boston of their post secondary education and formation in seminary.* PhD thesis, Boston College.

Cohen, L., & Felson, M. (1979). Social change and crime rate trends: A routine activities approach. *American Sociological Review, 44*, 588–607.

Cooperative Congregations Studies Partnership. (2010). Faith communities today: 2010 national survey of congregants. Hartford, CT, USA. Retrieved December 9, 2018 from http://faithcommunitiestoday.org/sites/faithcommunitiestoday.org/files/2010FrequenciesV1.pdf.

Daniel, K. (2012). The psychology behind celibacy. *International Journal of Psychology and Behavioral Sciences, 2*(4), 88–93. https://doi.org/10.5923/j.ijpbs.20120204.03.

Denney, A. S. (2015). Sex offenses at protestant Christian churches: A typology and examination using social disorganization theory. *Electronic Theses and Dissertations.* Paper 2102. https://doi.org/10.18297/etd/2102.

Denney, A., Kerkey, K., & Gross, N. (2018). Child sexual abuse in protestant christian congregations: A descriptive analyses of offense and offender characteristics. *Religions, 9*(27), 1–13.

Doyle, T. (2006). Clericalism: Enable of clerical sexual abuse. *Pastoral Psychology, 54*(3). https://doi.org/10.1007/s11089-006-6323-x.

Francis, P. C., & Baldo, T. D. (1998). Narcissistic measures of Lutheran clergy who self-reported committing sexual misconduct. *Pastoral Psychology, 47*, 81–96.

Flynn, K. A. (2003). *The sexual abuse of women by members of the clergy.* Jefferson, NC: McFarland & Co.

Friberg, N. C., & Laaser, M. R. (1998). *Before the fall: Preventing pastoral sexual abuse.* Collegeville: The Liturgical Press.

Garland, D. R., & Argueta, C. (2010). How clergy sexual misconduct happens: A qualitative study of first-hand accounts. *Social Work & Christianity, 37*, 1–27.

Gove, W. R., & Crutchfield, R. D. (1982). The family and juvenile delinquency. *Sociological Quarterly, 23*(3), 301–319.

Grammich, C. (2012). *Sources of change in catholic populations, 2000 to 2010.* Paper presented at the Joint Annual Meeting of the Religious Research Association and Society for the Scientific Study of Religion, Phoenix, AZ.

Greely, A. (2004). *Priests: A calling in crisis.* Chicago: University of Chicago Press.

Greely, A. (2003, February 10). The times and sexual abuse by priests. *America: The Jesuit Review.* https://www.americamagazine.org/issue/421/article/times-and-sexual-abuse-priests.

Granovetter, M. S. (1982). The strength of weak ties: A network theory revisited. In P. V. Mardsen & N. Lin (Eds.), *Social structure and network analysis* (pp. 105–130). Thousand Oaks, CA: Sage Publications.

Hirschi, T. (1969). *Causes of delinquency.* Berkeley: University of California Press.

Hoge, D. R. (2002). *The first five years of priesthood: A study of newly ordained Catholic priests.* MN: Liturgical Press.

Horst, E. A. (2000). *Questions and answers about clergy sexual misconduct.* Collegeville, MN: The Liturgical Press.

Issaco, A., Sahler, E., & Krinock, E. (2015). How religious beliefs and practices influence the psychological health of Catholic priests. *American Journal of Men's Health.* https://doi.org/10.1177/1557988314567325.

John Jay College of Criminal Justice. (2004). The nature and scope of sexual abuse of minors by Catholic priests and Deacons in the United States 1950–2002. Washington, D.C.: USCCB. http://www.bishop-accountability.org/reports/2004_02_27_JohnJay/.

Juang, L. P., & Silbereisen, R. K. (1999). Supportive parenting and adolescent adjustment across time in former East and West Germany. *Journal of Adolescence, 22*(6), 719–736.

Kasarda, J. D., & Morris, J. (1974). Community attachment in mass society. *American Sociological Review, 39*, 328–339.

Kornhauser, R. (1978). *Social sources of delinquency: An appraisal of analytic models*. Chicago, IL: University of Chicago Press.

Kubrin, C. E., & Weitzer, R. (2003). New directions in social disorganization theory. *Journal of Research in Crime and Delinquency*. https://doi.org/10.1177/0022427803256238.

Louden, S. H., & Francis, L. J. (2003). *The naked parish priest: What priests really think they're doing*. London & New York: Continuum.

Marshall, W. L., Serran, G. A., & Marshall, L. E. (2006). Situational and dispositional factors in child sexual molestation: A clinical perspective. In R. Wortley & S. Smallbone (Eds.), *Crime prevention studies* (Vol. 19, pp. 37–64)., Situational prevention of child sexual abuse Monsey, NY: Criminal Justice Press.

Martin, J. (2017, December 15). It's not about celibacy: Blaming the wrong thing for sexual abuse in the church. *America: the Jesuit Review*.

Meehan, M. P., Durlak, J. A., & Bryant, F. B. (1993). The relationship of social support to perceived control and subjective mental health in adolescents. *Journal of Community Psychology, 21*, 49–55.

Muse, J. S. (1992). Faith, hope, and the "urge to merge" in pastoral ministry: Some countertransference related distortions of relationships between male pastors and their female parishioners. *Journal of Pastoral Care, 46*(3), 299–308.

Owen, H. L. (2001, October). When did the Catholic Church decide priests should be celibate? *History News Network*. https://historynewsnetwork.org/article/696.

Pew Research Center. (2007). *Religion and public life project: Religious landscape survey*. Retrieved March 15, 2018, from: http://www.pewforum.org/religious-landscape-study/.

Plante, T. G. (2003). Psychological consultation with the Roman Catholic Church: Integrating who we are and what we do. *Journal of Psychology and Christianity, 22*, 304–308.

Plante, T. G., & Aldridge, A. (2005). Pschological patterns among Roman Catholic clergy accused of sexual misconduct. *Pastoral Psychology, 54*(1), 73–80. https://doi.org/10.1007/s11089-005-6184-8.

Poling, N. W. (1999). *Victim to survivor: Women recovering from clergy sexual abuse*. Cleveland: United Church Press.

Putnam, R. D. (2000). *Bowling alone*. New York: Simon & Schuster.

Rausch, T. P. (1992). *Priesthood today*. New York: Paulist Press.

Reis, A. Jr. (1986). Why are communities important in understanding crimes? In A. J. Reis, & M. Tonry (Eds.), *Communities and crimes* (pp. 1–33). Chicago: University of Chicago Press.

Rose, D. (2000). Social disorganization and social control: Religious institutions and their communities. *Sociological Forum, 15*(2), 339–358.

Rosetti, S. (2002, April 22). Five misconceptions abuse child sexual abuse and the Catholic Church. *America: The Jesuit Review*. https://www.americamagazine.org/politics-society/2002/04/22/five-misconceptions-about-child-sexual-abuse-and-catholic-church.

Sampson, R. J., & Groves, W. B. (1989). Community structure and crime: Testing social-disorganization theory. *American Journal of Sociology, 94*, 774–802.

Sampson, R. J., & Raudenbush, S. W. (1999). Systematic social observation of public spaces: A new look at disorder in urban neighborhoods. *American Journal of Sociology, 105*, 603–651.

Sampson, R. J., Raudenbush, S. W., & Earls, F. (1997). Neighbourhoods and violent crime: A multi level study of collective efficacy. *Science, 227*, 916–924.

Sampson, R. J., Morenoff, J. D., & Earls, F. (1999). Beyond social capital: Spatial dynamics of collective efficacy for children. *American Sociological Review, 64*, 633–660.

Schoenherr, R., & Vilarino, J. V. (1979). Organizational role commitment in the catholic church in spain and in the USA. In D. Hickson, & C. Lammers, (Eds.), *Organizations alike and unlike: International and inter-institutional studies in sociology of organizations* (pp. 346–372). London: Routledge & Kegan Paul.

Simons, R. L., Robertson, J. F., & Downs, W. R. (1989). The nature of the association between parental rejection and delinquent behavior. *Journal of Youth and Adolescence, 18*(3), 297–310.

Sharma, R. K. (2007). *Social change and social control*. New Delhi: Atlantic.

Shaw, C., & McKay, H. (1942). *Juvenile delinquency and urban areas*. Chicago: Chicago University Press.

Sheldrake, P. (1994). Celibacy and clerical culture. *The Way Supplement, 77*. Retrieved December 28, 2018 from https://www.theway.org.uk/back/s077Sheldrake.pdf.

Stark, R. (1987). Deviant places: A theory of the ecology of crime. *Criminology, 25*, 893–909.

Sunardi, Y. (2014). Predictive factors for commitment to the priestly vocation: A study of priests and seminarians. *Dissertations*. Paper 421. http://epublications.marquette.edu/dissertations_mu/421.

Swenson, D. (1998). Religious differences between married and celibate clergy: Does celibacy make a difference? *Sociology of Religion, 59*(1), 37–43. http://www.jstor.org/stable/3711964.

Sipe, A. W. R. (1990). *A secret world: Celibacy and the search for celibacy*. New York: Brunner/Mazel.

Sipe, A. W. R. (2010, April 28). Secret sex in the celibate system. *National Catholic Reporter*. https://www.ncronline.org/blogs/examining-crisis/secret-sex-celibate-system.

Thoburn, J., & Mitchell Whitman, D. (2004). Clergy affairs: Emotional investment, longevity of relationship and affair partners. *Pastoral Psychology, 52*, 491–506.

Thrasher, F. (1963). *The gang: A study of 1,313 gangs in Chicago, rev. ed.* Chicago: Chicago University Press.

Umberson, D. (1987). Family status and health behaviors: Social control as a dimension of social integration. *Journal of Health and Social Behavior, 28*(3), 306–319.

Virginia, S. G. (1998). Burnout and depression among Roman Catholic secular, religious, and monastic clergy. *Pastoral Psychology, 47*, 49–67.

Voorhis, P. V., Cullen, F. T., Mathers, R. A., & Garner, C. C. (1988). The impact of family structure on quality of delinquency: A comparative assessment of structural and functional factors. *Criminology. 26*(2), 235–261.

Wortley, R., & Smallbone, S. (2006). Applying situational principles to sexual offenses against children. In R. Wortley, & S. Smallbone (Eds.), *Situational prevention of child sexual abuse. Crime prevention studies* (Vol. 19). Monsey: Criminal Justice Press.

Chapter 5
Lay Empowerment, Social Disorganization, and Clerical Sexual Abuse

Abstract Using the sociological perspective and secondary literature, this chapter analyzes the role of the laity in the social organization of the Catholic hierarchy as a clerical community and social control of clerical behavior against sexual abuse. It stresses the need for lay empowerment in the behavioral monitoring of priestly conduct by allowing the laity to participate in the formal governance of the Catholic Church and oversee the social welfare of clerics in the hierarchy. Applying the social disorganization theory, it examines the renewed teaching of the Second Vatican Council on lay empowerment and participation in the Church and critically evaluates it whether it constitutes a substantial empowerment which bestows on the laity sufficient ecclesiastical power and authority to monitor the social networks of diocesan clergy against clerical sexual abuse. It also relates lay empowerment to the current social disorganization of the hierarchy and persistence of clerical sexual misconduct in the Church. It argues that an empowered laity can lead to increased intermediary social networks, cohesiveness, and social control of the Catholic hierarchy against clerical sexual abuse.

Introduction

The social disorganization theory (SDT) and the social network theory (SNT) in Sociology view the crucial role of mediating bodies in providing formal and informal social controls between various social networks of a community to resist crime and deviance. The absence of such bodies or organizations can lead to social disorganization and a prevalence of crime in an organization. The Roman Catholic Church (RCC) as a universal community of Christian believers has three types of members, namely: clerics, religious, and laity. Church documents emphasize the unity of the RCC as one "People of God" with interconnecting networks of bishops, priests, religious, and laity under the leadership of the pope.

Maintaining the unity of the universal Church has never been easy in actual social practice. Quite literally, the RCC faces a world of challenges within its own ranks. Roughly one billion persons across the globe call themselves Catholic, but they do so according to widely varying cultural viewpoints and individual experiences

(Marzheuser, 1995; Fitzpatrick, 1987). The RCC is composed of many local churches. But its leadership transcends the cultural diversity of its members. Over the course of centuries, the pope, bishops, and priests or what is collectively called as the Catholic hierarchy (CH) has served as a symbol and proponent of this desired unity. The pope in union with the college of bishops constitutes the ecclesiastical leadership which guides the RCC and is responsible for its adherence to "one Lord, one faith, one baptism (Schilling, 2002, p. 13).

But with the growing clerical sexual abuse (CSA) in the RCC around the globe involving priests and bishops of the Catholic hierarchy (CH), some lay Catholics begin to doubt this unity and cohesiveness of the clerical community. The pattern of bishops covering up CSA cases makes one wonders whether there is a strong control system of clerical behavior in the CH by members of the RCC called the laity.

In the midst of the continuing and widespread CSA, the laity stays passive in investigating and sanctioning predator priests in the RCC. Despite the renewed Church's teaching on lay empowerment and participation by the Second Vatican Council (Vatican II), lay Catholics still do not exercise administrative power to monitor, investigate, and prosecute erring priests in the Christian community. The RCC, being the largest Christian Church in the world with a population of more than one billion members, has the largest group of lay people which constitutes more than 99% of the church membership. Thus, one might ask why the laity, despite being the great majority of believers in the RCC, remains powerless in disciplining abusive members of the CH: Did Vatican II really provide lay Catholics real empowerment which is sufficient to address CSA?

Research studies which intend to understand the roots of CSA in the RCC have not so far examined the role of the laity in prosecuting CSA. Dominated by psychological and psychiatric perspectives, several studies on CSA primarily focus on the psychological, moral, and spiritual roots of the problem. Since 2002, much of the health-related scholarship about priests across disciplines, such as psychology and psychiatry, has mainly focused on identifying and preventing clergy sexual abuse of minors (e.g., John Jay College 2004, Plante 2003). It also anchors on the psychological profiles of predator priests as well as the negative effects of celibacy on the psychological health of priests. Some studies see the relationship between CSA and the weakening of lay influence in the RCC which resulted in clericalism (e.g., Doyle, 2006). Pscyho-social research on the well-being of priests began citing some situational and social factors that contribute to CSA (e.g., Rauch, 1992). What is apparently absent in all these studies is a structural analysis on the crucial role of the laity in providing formal and informal social controls to the CH to check clerical behavior, prevent sexual abuse, and investigate and process CSA cases. The sociological perspective which can provide a holistic view of the CSA problem is apparently neglected in the current research endeavors.

The CSA scandal did not only commence in the United States (US) with the Boston Globe's report on the molestation of 130 boys by John Geoghan of the RCC from 1962 until 1993. "Sexual abuse of people of any age and either sex by clergy has existed throughout the history of the Catholic Church" (Doyle, 2003, p. 190). In fact, there is a long history of ecclesiastical legal documentation by popes and the bishops from the fourth century up to the present against CSA.

In all media and public reports of sexual misconduct involving priests, what is apparently absent is the proactive participation of the laity in investigating, reporting, documenting, and penalizing abusive priests and bishops involved in CSA. Thus: Why are lay Catholics relatively passive in monitoring of clerical behavior as well as investigating and sanctioning clerical misconduct? Many CSA cases, especially against minors, could have been prevented if lay people are authorized to oversee clerical behavior, investigate sexual misconduct, or impose sanctions against predator priests.

Lay Empowerment in the Church

The universal council or assembly of all bishops with the Pope called the Second Vatican Council (Vatican II), which was convened by Pope John XXIII in October 1962, is widely seen by many as ushering a new era of reforms for the conservative church in the modern world. And one of the major reforms introduced by Vatican II is the adoption of *Apostolicam Actuositatem* (Apostolate of the Laity), a decree which called for lay empowerment and participation in the RCC. It encourages more involvement of the laity in the Church life. "The word laity derives from the Middle English laite, which ultimately stems from the Greek laikós (λαϊκός), meaning common or (one) of the people. In the RCC, the word laity designates those believers who have not received the sacrament of orders and as a result are those who are not clerics (ordained ministers)" (Central Commission for the Revision of the Statutes of *Regnum Christi*, Sept 2014, p. 3).

Church authorities yielded more lay engagement in the RCC with *Apostolicam Actuositatem*. But Vatican II's dogmatic constitution on the church, *Lumen Gentium* (Light of the World), reaffirmed the hierarchical structure of the RCC and enjoined the laity to accept the decisions of their pastors and bishops with "Christian obedience."[1] Thus, despite the good intentions of the RCC to empower the laity, the fact remains that lay Catholics still assume the secondary role in ecclesiastical affairs, separated from the ordained priests and bishops who are considered as "spiritual leaders" and "rulers" of the RCC:

> The laity [...] should openly reveal to them [spiritual shepherds] their needs and desires with that freedom and confidence which is fitting for children. [...] The laity should [...] promptly accept in Christian obedience decisions of their spiritual shepherds, since they are representatives of Christ as well as teachers and rulers in the Church of God and brothers in Christ. [...] Let the spiritual shepherds recognize and promote the dignity as well as the responsibility of the laity in the Church [...], allowing them freedom and room for action. Further, let them encourage lay people so that they may undertake tasks on their own initiative (*Lumen Gentium* #37).

---

[1] Peter J. Nixon, "The great awakening: How lay people have shaken up the church", Retrieved 28 May 2017, http://www.uscatholic.org/church/2010/07/great-awakening.

While this text suggests somewhat equal collaboration, the terminology of "children" for the laity and "rulers" for the clergy indicates a strong notion of inequality of position in the RCC between the clergy and laity as well as the subordination of the laity to their ordained shepherds. This is expected with the growing Catholic population and bureaucracy of the RCC as an institution in contemporary times and with the retention of the hierarchical structure. Although lay people can now take more tasks in the RCC with their own initiatives, *Lumen Gentium* still considers the ordained clerics as rulers and spiritual leaders in the ecclesiastical community.

The clergy still controls and governs the official Church. To participate in the formal governance of the RCC requires the reception of the sacrament of the holy orders. In the RCC, the power to govern the institution implies ordination to the priesthood and adoption of celibacy. Canon 129.1 says: "In accord with the prescription of law, those who received sacred orders are capable of the power of governance, which exists in the Church by divine institution and is also called the power of jurisdiction." Canon 129.2 also states that the laity only plays the secondary role of coordinating in the governance of the clergy: "Lay members of the Christian faithful can cooperate in the exercise of this power in accord with the norm of law".[2]

The passivity of the laity and growing dominance of the clerics in the Church administration started during the Constantine era and increased during the feudal and medieval periods. Eventually, the Council of Trent legitimized the separation between the clergy and laity and retained in present times despite Vatican II's modernizing reforms. The laity is still excluded from all acts of governance in the RCC. Clerics continue to be the Church's rulers and lay people as followers and collaborators. The clerical control remains dominant in the RCC after Vatican II. That is why in the minds of most Catholics the term 'the Church' is synonymous with the CH. In the current social structure of Church administration, which is supported by the Code of Canon Law (CCL), lay people are seen as passive recipients of the hierarchy's ministry.[3] Indeed, there are some instances that lay people initiate in some pastoral programs without the explicit approval of bishops and parish priests. But these initiatives are not decision-making processes which affect the official Church but apostolic endeavors that lay people can do as part of their Christian duties in the RCC.

The universal Catechism of the Catholic Church (CCC) also separates the laity from the clergy and professed religious. It defines the laity as "all the faithful except those in Holy Orders and those who belong to a religious state approved by the Church. That is, the faithful, who by Baptism are incorporated into Christ and integrated into the People of God, are made sharers in their particular way in the priestly, prophetic, and kingly office of Christ, and have their own part to play in the mission of the whole Christian people in the Church and in the World (CCC # 897)."[4] The Catholic laity is the baptized members who are neither ordained ministers nor

---

[2]Russell Shaw, *Nothing to Hide: Secrecy, Communication and Communion in the Catholic Church.* Ignatius Press. p. 159.

[3]Ibid.

[4]Catechism of the Catholic Church, 897, Retrieved 28 May 2017, "http://www.vatican.va/archive/ccc_css/archive/catechism/p123a9p4.htm.

professed vows as religious nuns, brothers, or priests in the RCC. It comprises more than 99% of the total Catholic population with only 0.5% as clerics and 1.5% as religious."[5]

Shifting the focus of the ecclesial image of the Church as People of God, Vatican II is perceived by many as bestowing on the laity more power and participation in the RCC. It had, for the first time, affirmed certain rights and responsibilities of the laity. Among these is the right and duty to make known their concerns to pastors and bishops. This right was later added to the CCL:

> According to the knowledge, competence, and prestige which [the laity] possess, they have the right and even at times the duty to manifest to the sacred pastors their opinion on matters which pertain to the good of the Church and to make their opinion known to the rest of the Christian faithful, without prejudice to the integrity of faith and morals, with reverence toward their pastors, and attentive to common advantage and the dignity of persons (Canon 212, 3).

Although these rights of the laity are recognized by the CH, there are no ecclesiastical structures to guarantee that they will be accepted or respected by the official Church.[6] Among the laity, there remains a fundamental lack of understanding of the lay vocation and its role in the Church's mission. Many lay Catholics still associate "the Church" with the ordained office and believe that only priests and religious are official providers of ecclesiastical service. They still think that the role of the laity is to help out around the parish and that they are not called to play an integral part in the mission of the Church. Canon 212, 3 of the CCL, for instance, speaks only of the rights of the laity to manifest their opinion on matters which pertain to the good of the RCC. But these rights do not include participation in the decision-making process of the official Church. Vatican II may be promoting lay empowerment, but the CCL is still insisting that the rights of the laity only pertain to giving suggestions, collaborating, or coordinating with the clergy on apostolic matters. Thus, the ordained clerics still rule the RCC and exercise discretionary power on whether to accept or reject the laity's suggestions or initiatives on ecclesiastical matters.

Understanding Empowerment

Many Catholics view Vatican II as radical in advancing the idea of lay empowerment since it advocates the idea of the priesthood of all believers which is now being fully incorporated into the Catholic ecclesiology. The laity is now acknowledged as full members of the RCC and as priests like the ordained clergy (Weidner, 2017). With this development, many clergy and Catholic laity hoped that the power of clericalism would wane, especially in light of Vatican II's emphasis on the role of lay members in Church life (Cullinane, 1997). Despite the wide acceptance of the renewed lay

---

[5]Leonard Doohan, "Lay People and the Church", Retrieved 28 May 2017, http://www.theway.org.uk/Back/32Doohan.pdf. pp. 169–174.

[6]"Church Governance", http://www.votf.org/Structural_Change/ChurchGovernance-VOTF.pdf.

involvement in the RCC after Vatican II, the present generation of young priests still views themselves as essentially different from the laity and as men set apart by God (Hoge, 2002).

A close sociological scrutiny of Vatican II's teaching on lay empowerment, however, reveals a different story. The concept of a shared priesthood of Christ by all members of the RCC still shows a great difference between the priesthood of the laity and that of the clergy. Although conciliar documents perceive the laity as sharing in priesthood of Christ together with the ordained clergy, the official Church still accepts the two types of the priesthood in the RCC's social structure: general priesthood of the laity and ministerial priesthood of the CH.

The laity's priesthood, on the one hand, is a general character in which all members of the RCC, whether clergy, religious or lay, share by virtue of the common baptism in the Church. But this priesthood does not confer on the laity the sacramental and political powers of the RCC. The clerical priesthood, on the other hand, is a specialized one with sacramental and administrative powers to govern the internal affairs of the official Church. The former only grants the power of coordination and collaboration with the clergy in Church affairs, but the latter bestows on the candidates the power and authority to directly govern the Church bureaucracy.

From a sociological perspective, Vatican II's lay empowerment and extension of the priesthood to the laity did not really result in a substantial power-sharing between the laity and the clergy. In sociology of power, empowerment is understood as a political process. At the center of the concept of empowerment is the idea of power. The essence of empowerment lies in the dynamics of distribution and redistribution of power. Empowerment requires that power must change. If power cannot change and inherent in positions or people, then empowerment is not possible, nor is empowerment conceivable in any meaningful way (Page and Czuba, 1999). In short, if power is shared from one person or group to another, there is a meaningful empowerment.

Analyzing lay empowerment requires an investigation whether the RCC's renewed teaching on lay empowerment includes sharing of ecclesiastical power from the clergy to the laity. Power, according to the German sociologist Max Weber, is the ability to make others do what one wants, regardless of their own wishes or interests (Weber, 1946). And when this capacity to control is legitimized, it becomes authority. Hence empowerment will mean a process of distribution of power through legitimized means. Ultimately, empowerment implies the sharing of authority in the political structure of an institution. In the case of RCC, empowerment would imply sharing and delegating some of the clerics' political and ecclesiastical powers to the non-ordained members of the RCC, especially to the laity which constitutes the vast majority of the RCC's members.

"For to empower all involves shedding power by the few who traditionally exercised it exclusively. This touches not only on who has a public ministry or access to theological education but also to the continued absence of married experience among established decision-makers" (Sheldrake, 1994, p. 33). The CCL–despite Vatican II's renewed emphasis on lay empowerment–still exclusively reserves the ecclesiastical authority and control of the official Church to the celibate clergy. Thus, it becomes doubtful whether there can be a meaningful lay empowerment after Vatican II if positions of power and authority in the RCC are not directly shared or delegated from the clergy to the laity.

"The complex link between celibacy and power is part of the reason why, despite changes in theory since Vatican II, the institution of the Church still finds the actual empowerment of all its members difficult" (Sheldrake, 1994). Clerical training and Church governance are still reserved for the celibate CH. At present, there is no substantial sharing of ecclesiastical authority from the clergy to the laity, especially in addressing and sanctioning CSA. Lay Catholics are still not appointed, for example, to political positions in the Church's highest governing body–the Roman Curia, as top administrators in tasks which may not even need expertise in theology or canon law. They cannot even make independent decisions in diocesan and pastoral councils without the approval of the bishops and parish priests. In addition, no lay persons are allowed to participate as policy-makers in the major legislative and consultative assemblie, and policy-making bodies of the RCC such as ecumenical and local councils, the synod of bishops, and bishops' conferences. The laity may be consulted for their expertise on secular matters by the CH but they could not make political decisions on internal matters in the RCC.

The RCC has not changed its fundamental political structure and governance system after Vatican II. Canon law continues to provide bishops absolute rule in the diocese, liable only to the pope, just as the parish priest has an absolute rule in the parish life, liable only to the bishop. The fact remains that only the ordained ministers have total control of the decision-making process in the RCC. Lay people are only given more areas of participation in the pastoral and apostolic life of their respective dioceses and parishes with Vatican II's concept of lay empowerment.

Albeit the current Catholic teaching on lay involvement insists that lay people have their own realm of apostolic ministry and not merely participating in the apostolate of the CH because of their expertise on secular matters, the internal management of the Church bureaucracy continues to be exercised exclusively by the clergy. Still, only parish priests and bishops possess ecclesiastical authority and supervision of the RCC under the CCL. Regulating clerical behavior remains an exclusive duty of the CH. The laity can only report CSA cases to Church authorities but it is ultimately the bishops who have the power to investigate and decide abuse cases with the discretion to report them or not to the Sacred Congregation of the Doctrine of the Faith (CDF) of the Roman Curia for sanction.[7]

In sum, Vatican II and the current Church's view on lay empowerment is only an enlargement of the laity's participation in the apostolic affairs of the Christian community, but not in the internal management of the RCC. Despite the claims of sharing one priesthood of Christ by all members of the Church and lay empowerment, the laity remains mere followers of the clerics and passive recipients of the CH's ministry. The ordained ministers or the clergy still assumes political leadership in the official Church, although the laity is given more apostolic responsibilities. Decision-making and ecclesial authority are still reserved to ordained bishops and priests by the CCL. Thus, there was no real empowerment of the laity in the sociological sense of power-sharing in Church governance after Vatican II. The hierarchical structure is preserved by the council with the clergy occupying at the top of the pyramid as the "ruling elite" of the RCC, followed by the consecrated religious and laity as subjects and followers of the CH. The laity occupies the lowest stratum in the social stratification of the RCC. The CCL is still explicit that only ordained clerics have the special power to occupy offices in the Church (Canon 274,1) that the religious and the laity must obey the CH.

This prominence of the clergy in the social structure of the RCC has the negative unintended effect of clericalism, that is, a cultural perception that clerics constitute the political elite in the Church, a special group of people who are set apart from the laity by virtue of ordination. Doyle (2006) views clericalism as the radical misunderstanding of the place of clerics (deacons, priests, bishops) in the RCC and in the secular society that fundamentally distorts, disrupts, and poisons the Christian lives of members of the church and weakens the church in her mission to the world.

Implication of Limited Lay Empowerment to Clerical Behavior

One indicator that a community is having a social disorganization problem is the lack of formal and informal social controls that monitor deviance or crime committed by community members (e.g., Kapsis 1976, Simcha-Fagan and Schwartz 1986, Skogan 1986, Khron 1986). To increase the social control of a certain community requires strong social ties and supervision of other groups within the community to increase behavioral regulation to discourage crime and deviance. The RCC as a Christian community is composed of three general types of members: clerics and religious which constitute around one percent of the total population and laity which comprises more than ninety-nine percent of the entire membership. To increase social control

---

[7]The CDF is the Vatican's main watchdog on issues of church doctrine and on investigation of serious crimes within the church. It is has the final authority with the papal approval to defrock or remove a bishop, priest, or deacon as a member of the hierarchy for serious crimes committed in the church.

against CSA within the Christian community requires a strong lay participation in the life of the CH, giving lay Catholics more authority and power to supervise priestly behavior and intervene in internal ecclesiastical affairs and, when necessary, to investigate and prosecute abusive priests and bishops in the RCC. As members, the RCC through its official documents (e.g., *Lumen Gentium* 31; *Christifideles Laici* 2; *Catechism of the Catholic Church* 898) have already acknowledged the secular vocation of the laity and their active role to play in the Church (*Decree on the Apostolate of the Laity*, 10; *Catechism of the Catholic Church* 900); thus, lay Catholics are in a better structural position to proactively check CSA and prosecute erring priests in collaboration with the CH officials.

The inability of the CH to address and overcome the widespread CSA and patterns of covering-up sexual abuse cases makes one thinks whether the current structure of the clergy is socially disorganized–without other systems of checks and balances from other members of the RCC such as the religious and the laity. The RCC as a community of believers ought to be cohesive as taught by Church documents with the clerics, religious, and laity coordinating with one another to inhibit crime and deviance within the Christian community. But with the growing CSA scandals in RCC, this ideal is far from the social reality. Empirically, the structural dimensions of social disorganization are measured by scholars in terms of the prevalence and inter-dependence of social networks in the community–both informal (e.g., friendship ties) and formal (e.g., organizational participation)–and in the span of collective super-vision that the community directs toward local problems (Thomas and Znanaiecki, 1920; Shaw and McKay, 1942; Kornhauser, 1978). But with the atomized relation-ship between the clergy, religious, and laity in the RCC's social structure, a strong interdependence and social networking between different types of Church members that strengthen the collective action against CSA would be difficult.

Although Church documents posit unity of all Church believers, the dominance of one group over other groups would imply social disorganization and weak behav-ioral monitoring and networking between the clergy, religious, and laity against CSA. One group such as the laity cannot directly monitor against abusive conduct of erring members of the CH without authority from the official Church. Despite the lay empowerment after Vatican II, there is no significant lay empowerment and substan-tial sharing of power and authority because of the current hierarchical structure of the Church that concentrates ecclesiastical powers only to the clerics. Even appointments to certain top positions in the RCC which deal with non-doctrinal and sacramental matters such as heads or administrators of top judicial and investigative bodies of the in Rome and dioceses against CSA remains difficult to access for responsible and highly qualified lay leaders. With the universal mandatory celibacy for clerics and monarchical powers of the bishops, the laity could not assume political positions in the RCC to prevent CSA.

The CCL has clearly reserved the power of ecclesiastical governance to the CH, making it difficult for the laity and religious to network with the clergy for purposes of regulating priestly behavior and increasing social controls against CSA. One case of a bishop in India who had been repeatedly raping a religious nun can be a classic example. The religious order could not directly investigate and sanction the bishop for his crime nor immediately file charges against him in civil court being a Church leader and a member of the CH. The poor victim had to exert extra effort to report the bishop to the police and charge him with rape. There is no clear mechanism in the local church to directly held him accountable for his deeds before the civil authorities could interfere in the case.

The lack of power to investigate the clerical life of the CH for purposes of providing support and strengthening its ecclesiastical social control against CSA is even more apparent between the laity and clergy. As revealed by various investigative reports on child sexual abuse by the clergy, the laity is powerless to prosecute abuse cases within the RCC, given the monarchial powers of the bishops in the CH to discipline priests. Thus, several abuse cases are unreported to the official Church or reported when the victims have already reached adulthood. Many of these cases are also amicably settled by bishops with the victims to avoid public scandals.

Investigations on CSA revealed a socially disorganized or loosely networked clerical life of the CH with bishops and priests living autonomous lives with total privacy in their personal affairs, without the benefit of an effective behavioral review by the laity to enhance clerical accountability. Currently, the CH lacks direct and indirect social controls from other Church members to monitor and prevent CSA. Unrestrained behavior has always been seen by sociologists as prone to deviance and criminality. And social disorganization and network theorists often see the lack of bridging social networks and intermediary bodies that connect the various groups in a community as necessary to increase social ties and social control to against crime.

Conversely, there are no effective lay intermediary groups that monitor the decisions and actions of the CH and between bishops and the Roman Curia and between the pope and bishops around the world. This is the reason why newly ordained diocesan priests aspire to become members of religious associations or groups for mutual support. Since only ordained ministers can participate in ecclesiastical governance, lay organizations can only advise or suggest the CH on how to deal with CSA but could not participate directly in prosecuting abusive clerics in the Church. In the Holy See, lay people can only participate in investigations and giving of recommendations to the Roman Curia concerning CSA with the appointment and approval of the pope. Except for the broadcast and social media which sometimes scrutinize the affairs of the Vatican, there is no stable formal and informal structures that allow lay people to monitor the CH and Roman Curia for any wrongdoing or cover-up involving CSA.

Lay Empowerment and Participation in the Diocese and Parish

In the diocesan and parish levels, there are opportunities for the lay Catholics to participate in the activities of the CH and recommend policies for the good of the Church's apostolate. But they could not censure bishops and members of the clergy without the consent of the pope or local ordinaries. Membership of the laity in any diocesan or parochial board is not based on a random selection that reflects the different interests and concerns of Catholics in the diocese or parish. Official Church documents state that the Pastoral Councils represent the people of God, but not in the legal sense. Rather, council members are representatives in that they are as a witness or a sign of the whole community. They make its wisdom present (Sacred Congregation for the Clergy, Private letter on Pastoral Councils, #7). The Pastoral Council is a representative body rather than a body of representatives. A council member is not a representative for a particular neighborhood, age bracket, special interest group or organization.

The laity has no control in the selection of parish pastoral councils. The CCL provides for the formation of Parish Pastoral Councils (PPCs) which entirely depends on the decision of the local bishop and parish priest. Canon 536, 1 of the CCL states: In every parish of the diocese, a Pastoral Council shall be established, if the diocesan Bishop, after consulting with the Council of Presbyters, allows it. The pastor presides over the Pastoral Council. The Pastoral Council is composed of members of the congregation together with those of the parish staff who have pastoral care by reason of their office. One parish of a diocese in the US clearly shows that the PPC's role does not include sharing in the formal governance of the parish and monitoring of clerical behavior but only advising and helping the parish priest in the apostolate and activities of the parish:

> Section I: Purpose The role of the Parish Advisory Board is to advise and to assist the Pastor and his Parochial Vicar(s) in: 1) Formulating and implementing a community set-ting that promotes spiritual growth and formation, spiritual instruction, social education, works of charity, and recreational activities of the parish. 2) Formulating and implement-ing fund-raising programs to clear all debts of the parish and to finance spiritual, social, charitable, and recreational activities as set forth above. 3) The administration and physical maintenance/appearance of the parish.[8]

The Pastoral Council can only assist the parish priest or parochial vicar concerning the spiritual growth, social education, charity, and other apostolic work of the parish. It could not participate in the ecclesiastical decision-making of the parish. The PPC is dependent on the parish priest. Every recommendation needs his approval. Thus, any action of the lay parishioner that is critical of him could easily be denied. When a parish becomes vacant due to death, resignation, or transfer of the pastor, the current PPC ceases to function. A new parish priest can form a new PPC. In this case, the PPC has no canonical personality to govern the parish and can easily be overruled by the parish priest.

In the US, after clerical sexual scandals were exposed by the media, Catholic bishops were forced to give concessions and allowed the lay review boards, such as a national advisory board, to monitor the diocesan compliance on actions against pedophile priests. In the final analysis, given the canonical restrictions which require all laity to serve only in an advisory capacity, credibility and trust can only be restored only if bishops allow lay advisory boards to be truly policy-making bodies

---

[8]"St. Joseph Advisory Board Constitution and By-Laws. Retrieved 28 May 2017, http://www. stjosephcctx.org/bylaws.pdf.

or ecclesiastical enforcement boards. Under the current canonical structure, the lay advisory boards can only recommend to the CH on how to deal with CSA but could not directly impose formal sanctions against abusive priests. But bishops can ignore the laity's recommendations.[9]

In the absence of professional judicial system in the RCC, non-participation of the laity in the church decision-making process and the lack of informal controls by lay advisory boards or pastoral councils, the CH could not probably craft an adequate solution against the persistence of clerical abuse within their ranks and protect minors from CSA. Thus, the only recourse of the victims is to approach the civil authority for protection and justice.

Lay Empowerment and Clerical Sexual Abuse

The persistence of CSA in the CH reveals something that is beyond psychological and psychiatric problems of the Catholic secular clergy. It shows a structural flaw in the social control system of the RCC against CSA. It exposes a loophole in the system of checks and balances between the various types of social networks in the RCC.

Although the RCC teaches unity and communion of all Church members namely, the clergy, religious, and laity, as sharing the mission of Christ, the fact remains that each type of members live parallel lives. The powerful clerical group of the CH live unrestrained life without a behavioral regulation by the laity. So also the religious with their own spirituality and religious constitution, who are relatively independent from the clerics of the CH and laity albeit under the supervision of their generals and superiors of the religious orders or congregations and authorities of the Sacred Congregation for Religious in the Roman Curia. Clerics of the CH and religious constitute less than 1% of the total Church population, while the laity who are immersed in the secular world comprises more than 99% of the total Church members. The lack of political power of the laity to monitor clerical behavior lessens the social control and checks and balances of the CH against CSA and thus contributes to the social disorganization to the clerical community.

Central to SDT is the neighborhood mechanisms that reduce crime and disorder. Foremost among these are residents' social ties and the degree in which people exercise social control in their neighborhoods. Social ties and informal control are theorized as mediating the effects of exogenous sources of social disorganization. It also highlights informal control that includes residents' or community members' efforts to prevent or sanction disorderly and criminal conduct through formal and informal surveillance (Kubrin and Weitzer, 2003). Informal control has been traditionally theorized as an outcome of social ties (Bursik, 1988, p. 527). Thus, stronger

---

[9]"Bishops must give lay boards real authority", FutureChurch, Retrieved 28 May 2017, https://www.futurechurch.org/press-releases/bishops-must-give-lay-boards-real-authority. "St. Joseph Advisory Board Constitution and By-Laws. Retrieved 28 May 2017, http://www.stjosephcctx.org/bylaws.pdf.

social ties within a community increase informal social control against crime and deviance. The SDT recognizes the need for various intermediary social networks to provide formal and informal social controls to prevent the persistence of abuse in a community.

Strengthening social ties in a community is crucial in preventing crime. Thus, a universal married priesthood or optional clerical celibacy and strong lay empowerment are important factors to combat CSA in the CH. Married priesthood can create familial ties and friendship networks, formal and informal associations or groups among spouses, children, and relatives of married clergy in the CH and can lead to greater social control of clerical behavior as well as opportunities for lay participation in ecclesiastical governance. Lay networks of married clergy can now provide a firm direct and indirect supervision of clerical behavior which can increase guardianship against CSA. This is not possible under the current form of lay empowerment and obligatory clerical celibacy. Some early SDT studies assumed that social ties and social control shaped crime rates. Sampson and Groves (1989) argued that local friendship networks, participation in formal and voluntary organizations, and a community's ability to supervise and control group behavior explain much of the effect of exogenous characteristics on crime and victimization.

Most of the CSA cases brought to Church authorities were initiated either by the victims or/and their relatives with the aid of mass media. Over the past fifteen years, there have been approximately 1800 civil suits and 200 civil and criminal trials involving various forms of CSA by Catholic clergy in the US. The civil suits are initiated by aggrieved laypersons such as victims and/or their parents against various religious communities or dioceses and bishops (Doyle, 2006, p. 191). In no way, lay pastoral or diocesan councils are proactively involved in investigating and mediating with the CH in behalf of the victims with a view of sanctioning the abusive priests.

When the widespread CSA in the US was first exposed to the public by the Boston Globe, research and investigation by the laity on nature and extent of clerical misconduct were only done after the United States Bishops Conference (USBC) commissioned a study in 2004. Lay parochial boards only started to cooperate in sexual abuse investigation after the approval of their respective bishops and after abuses cases have become public scandals and popular in broadcast and print media. A CSA investigation could not commence and progress in the RCC without the cooperation of the local bishops of the predator priests who, according to the CCL, possess the plenary power of disciplining erring secular clerics under their dioceses. Individually, each bishop serves as the religious leader, financial head, and political connection to the secular world in which the Catholic Church operates. All priests, nuns and others who work for the diocese are under his management and control.

Due to the lack of lay empowerment and exclusion of the laity from the formal Church administration, lay people cannot participate in direct regulation of clerical behavior and thus remain passive in the midst of a widening CSA. Lay Catholics, even though they are appointed as members of some diocesan and parochial boards, have no real administrative and coercive powers to prosecute erring priests in the Church's judicial system without the consent of the local bishops and the Roman Curia. The

RCC is governed only by a small group of all-male ordained clerics. Despite the significant progress done by Vatican II to empower the millions of non-ordained members of the RCC called the laity, lay participation in the formal leadership of the RCC remains missing.

Under the present ecclesiastical structure, lay people cannot formally regulate clerical behavior such as lifestyle check of clerics, initiating investigations against allegations of CSA, and prosecuting abusive priests in the ecclesiastical judicial bodies. In short, the laity has no direct and formal authority to discipline priests to deal with CSA cases. Abusive priests are only liable to their bishops, while abusive bishops are only liable to the Pope, thus sidelining millions of lay Catholics around the world, who are geographically in the position to keep an eye of the priest's secular behavior and to track and identify CSA. Principal conciliar documents such as *Lumen Gentium* have already recognized the secular character of the laity as "fully immersed in the temporal affairs of the world" and, thus, more knowledgeable on how to identify clerical misconduct in the secular world.

In the wake of widespread CSA in the US and all over the world, there is a need for greater lay empowerment in the RCC. This implies sharing of ecclesiastical power from the CH to lay people, not just symbolic advisory positions, is urgently needed to monitor and prevent CSA. Lay empowerment with the power to make binding decisions in the RCC is now vital more than ever to address the social disorganization in the CH and resist the growing CSA in the RCC.

Summary

This chapter has shown that Vatican II's renewed teaching on lay empowerment and participation did not alter the basic political structure of the RCC where ordained priests and bishops still occupy the highest social stature and political positions in the CH, making them special rulers with the laity as supporters and followers, passive recipient of the CH's ministry. Vatican II's lay empowerment is only an expansion of the lay participation in the non-political affairs of the RCC and not in the area of power-sharing or distribution of authority from the clergy to the laity in the official Church. The governance of the RCC is still reserved to the clergy according to CCL. In all CSA cases, the laity generally plays a passive role. Only bishops of the CH have the power to investigate and decide CSA cases. The lack of lay empowerment can contribute to the social disorganization of the CH. Clerical behavior can be restrained to prevent CSA by intermediary groups and familial networks if married priesthood is allowed in the RCC, creating more formal and informal social ties and more opportunities for the laity to participate in decision-making processes and governance of the RCC.

References

Bursik, Robert J. (1988). Social disorganization and theories of crime and delinquency: Problems and prospects. *Criminology, 26,* 519–551.

Cullinane, P. (1997). Clericalism: Avoidable damage to the Church. *Australasian Catholic Record, 76,* 181–197.

Doyle, T. P. (2003). Roman Catholic clericalism, religious duress, and clergy sexual abuse. *Pastoral Psychology, 51*(3).

Doyle, T. P. (2006). Clericalism: Enabler of clergy sexual abuse. *Pastoral Psychology, 54*(3), 189–213. https://doi.org/10.1007/s11089-006-6323-x.

Fitzpatrick, J. (1987). *One Church, many cultures: Challenge of diversity.* London: Sheed and Ward.

Hoge, D. (2002). *The first five years of priesthood: A study of newly ordained priests.* Collegeville, MN: Liturgical Press.

Kapsis, R. (1976). Continuities in delinquency and riot patterns in black residential areas. *Social Problems, 23,* 567–580.

Khron, M. (1986). The web of conformity: A network approach to the explanation of delinquent behavior. *Social Problems, 33,* 81–93.

Kornhauser, R. (1978). *Social sources of delinquency.* Chicago: Chicago University Press.

Kubrin, C. E., & Weitzer, R. (2003). New directions in social disorganization theory. *Journal of Research in Crime and Delinquency.* https://doi.org/10.1177/0022427803256238.

Marzheuser, R. (1995, December 5). Differing images of church. *America, 173*(18), 17–21.

Page, N., & Czuba, C. E. (1999). Empowerment: What is it? *The Journal of Extension, 37*(5).

Plante, T. G. (2003). Psychological consultation with the Roman Catholic Church: Integrating who we are and what we do. *Journal of Psychology and Christianity, 22,* 304–308.

Sampson, R. J., & Groves, W. B. (1989). Community structure and crime: Testing the social disorganization theory. *American Journal of Sociology, 94,* 774–802.

Schilling, T. P. (2002). *Conflict in the Catholic Hierarchy: A study of coping strategies in the Hunthausen Affair, with preferential attention to discursive strategies.* The Netherlands: Labor Grafimedia BV Utrecht.

Shaw, C., & McKay, H. (1942). *Juvenile delinquency and urban areas.* Chicago: Chicago University Press.

Sheldrake, P. (1994). Celibacy and clerical culture. *The Way Supplement, 77.* https://www.theway. org.uk/back/s077Sheldrake.pdf.

Simcha-Fagan, O., & Schwartz, J. E. (1986). Neighborhood and delinquency: An assessment of contextual effects. *Criminology, 24,* 667–703.

Skogan, W. (1986).Fear of crime and neighborhood change. In A. J. Reis, Jr. & M. Tomry (Eds.), *Communities and crime* (pp. 203–209). Chicago: Chicago University Press.

Thomas, W. I. & Znaniecki, F. (1920). *The polish peasant in Europe and America,* vol. 4. Boston: Gorham.

Weber, M. (1946). *From Max Weber.* H. H. Gerth & C. W. Mills (Eds.). New York: Oxford University Press.

Weidner, J. J. (2017). The priesthood of the laity. *Obsculta, 10*(1), 11–30. http://digitalcommons. csbsju.edu/obsculta/vol10/iss1/3.

Manufactured by Amazon.ca
Bolton, ON